The Book of Matthew

The Book of Matthew

The Story of a Learning-Disabled Child

Betty Jane Wylie

McClelland and Stewart

Copyright © 1984 by Betty Jane Wylie

Reprinted in paperback 1985

All rights reserved. The use of any part of this publication reproduced, transmitted in any form or by any means, electronic, mechanical, photocopying, recording, or otherwise, or stored in a retrieval system, without the prior consent of the publisher is an infringement of the copyright law.

The Canadian Publishers
McClelland and Stewart Limited
25 Hollinger Road, Toronto   M4B 3G2

Canadian Cataloguing in Publication Data

Wylie, Betty Jane, 1931–
    The book of Matthew

Bibliography: p.
ISBN 0-7710-9059-5 (bound).
ISBN 7710-9060-9 (pbk.)

1. Wylie, Matthew.   2. Developmentally disabled children – Biography.   3. Learning disabilities – Biography: I. Title.

HV891.W94 1984   155.4'516   C84-098876-1

Printed in Canada

To Matthew, of course, and all the people who have helped him

Other books by Betty Jane Wylie:

Beginnings: A Book for Widows
No Two Alike
Betty Jane's Diary: Lessons Children Taught Me
Everywoman's Money Book (with Lynne MacFarlane)

Cookbooks
Encore: The Leftovers Cookbook
The Betty Jane Wylie Cheese Cookbook

Children's Books
Don't Just Stand There – Jiggle!
Tecumseh
John of a Thousand Faces

Plays
The Horsburgh Scandal
The Old Woman and the Pedlar/Kingsayer
Mark
A Place on Earth

TABLE OF CONTENTS

CHAPTER ONE:	Learning Disability	9
CHAPTER TWO:	The Beginning	17
CHAPTER THREE:	The Learning Process	27
CHAPTER FOUR:	Therapy	37
CHAPTER FIVE:	Family	53
CHAPTER SIX:	Schooling	65
CHAPTER SEVEN:	Church, Camp, Community	81
CHAPTER EIGHT:	The Single Parent	93
CHAPTER NINE:	Epilepsy	101
CHAPTER TEN:	Persecution	113
CHAPTER ELEVEN:	Breakdown	121
CHAPTER TWELVE:	Life Goes On	133
CHAPTER THIRTEEN:	Group Homes and Alternatives	141
CHAPTER FOURTEEN:	Sex	155
CHAPTER FIFTEEN:	The Future	167
GLOSSARY		173
BIBLIOGRAPHY		177

CHAPTER ONE

LEARNING DISABILITY

You clutch at straws at first. You read every book you can lay your hands on searching for the magic key that will unlock the door to your child's future. You keep wishing—that's too weak a word— you keep *longing* for a miracle, for someone to say that in time everything will be "normal," that life will return to the way it was before this problem was dumped in your lap. It's not going to, ever. When you have a special child, there's no such thing as normal.

Few families are as fortunate as we were. We knew from the very beginning that we had trouble on our hands, and we were able to brace ourselves for it and try to do something about it immediately. A lot of parents are not aware for a long time that there is anything seriously wrong with their child. They may assume that he's slow because he's a first child and has no brothers or sisters to set him an example, or maybe he's lazy because he's a last child and doesn't have to try because everyone knows what he wants anyway. Or they comfort themselves by assuming that he's awkward because he's growing so fast, or that he's hyperactive because he feels insecure since both his parents are working and are too busy to pay him much attention, or maybe he's sulky and stubborn because he doesn't have enough playmates his own age to work off his energy with or learn to get along with, or maybe he's distractible because he has too many playmates and he gets too excited with them. The explanations, the denials, the anxieties, the questions, and the suspicions go on and on.

Right now, you may be wondering how special your child is. He may still be very young and not progressing the way you think he should, or not behaving the way your neighbour's child behaves. Or she may already be at school and called a behaviour problem. In any case, you have enough doubts about him or her and about yourself that you are beginning to search for help, reassurance, and – if you're lucky – maybe even a diagnosis.*

There are always explanations to be found before the facts must be faced. Even after the child starts school, teachers are reluctant to face the facts as well. Often they hope that he will "grow out of it" or that next year's teacher will be able to deal with him better.

Nagging doubts, repressed fears, and recurrent failures usually come long before diagnosis, and have their effect on the child's confidence and emotional balance before any remedies are attempted. "Why can't you pay attention? Why can't you sit still? Why don't you try harder?" He's had a lifetime of nagging and criticism thrown at him before anyone suggests that his behaviour may not be his fault, that his difficulties with learning are not due to stubbornness, laziness, or sheer stupidity.

Whatever learning problems the child has are quickly compounded by emotional problems: resentment, frustration, hopelessness. Add to that the pressure the adults are laying on him and the unerring ability of children to go for the jugular, and you have a very unhappy child.

"Hey, dummy! Re-tard, re-tard." The catcalls follow the kid into the playground and home from school. By grade one the class is divided into Bluebirds, Robins, Cardinals – or whatever names the teacher can think of – but the kids all know the Cardinals are the smartest, and by Christmas the poor Robins are still struggling to learn to read.

Long before then, Mother is spending extra time with the kid at home, trying to help him learn to read. Father despairs of his

---

* These days great care is usually taken to identify an unknown person equally as he/she. However, in this case, it really is a safe bet that the person we are talking about now is male. If there are not more defective males born than females – and statistics seem to show that there are – then the females manage to hide in the system better and are not caught out the way the boys are. Therefore, in this book I will refer to the learning disabled person as "he" for convenience.

ever learning to catch a ball. His brothers and sisters, if any, resent being told to wait for Jimmy.

The tension is not limited to the child by this time. Parents begin to tell each other that it comes from one or the other side of the family—dotty Uncle Ernie or dizzy Aunt Louise. Anxiety on the mother's part and shame on the father's (many men can't bear the idea that a son of theirs should be defective, less than perfect) have their effect on the marital relationship. As time goes on, there are extra financial burdens: special educational toys that might help, extra tutorial help, special diagnosis, a stab at a miracle treatment, anything that will assure the couple that Jimmy will be "okay." And if there are other children in the family, they will begin to be jealous of the extra time and attention Jimmy is getting from their parents.

As parents soon discover, school does not solve all the problems. That poor, overworked teacher seems as harassed and baffled by the kid as they are. Even when a teacher or a parent blows a whistle and asks for help, for tests, for diagnosis—and this doesn't happen automatically—the results are not always clear. Early assessments often put the blame squarely on the parents, especially the mother. ("If you'd stop fussing about him so much, he wouldn't have this problem." Listen, you wouldn't *be* fussing if he didn't have this problem.)

When a clear diagnosis finally comes, it's accepted almost with a sense of relief. Jimmy's "problem" at least has a label. He's not a product of neglect or bad parenting. After this, it's going to be easy, isn't it? It isn't. After this begins the difficulty of picking the intricate, damaged locks in Jimmy's brain in order to open it and teach him. And the damn thing is that by this time it may be almost too late. After nearly a decade in school (a lot of kids aren't "discovered" until they're almost finished—in every sense of the word), Jimmy may not want his locks picked. He's ready to quit. He gave up long ago.

This is just a very brief summary of the problems encountered when one has a damaged child—however damaged—and these days there are a lot of catch phrases used to dump a child in a reject file. Each case, of course, is terribly specific. Brain damage of any kind is capricious. It's like a case of faulty wiring. You turn the stove on but the bell rings or the oven door pops open. Short circuits abound, and no two cases are alike.

Here is the official definition of learning disabilities from the Ontario Ministry of Education:

A disorder evident in both academic and social situations that involves one or more of the processes necessary for the proper use of spoken language or the symbols of communication and that is characterized by a condition that:
a) is not primarily the result of
  i impairment of vision
  ii impairment of hearing
  iii physical handicap
  iv mental retardation
  v primary emotional disturbance, or
  vi cultural differences; and
b) results in a significant discrepancy between academic achievement and assessed intellectual ability with deficits in one or more of:
  i receptive language
  ii language processing
  iii expressive language
  iv mathematical computations; and
c) may be associated with one or more conditions diagnosed as:
  i perceptual handicap
  ii a brain injury
  iii dyslexia
  iv developmental aphasia.

The term itself — learning disability — is just about exactly as old as my son, and it is not yet used universally. Here are some of the other fashionable labels applied to the problem:

— brain damage
— (minimal) brain injury
— (minimal) neurological handicap
— hyperkinesis or hyperactivity
— perceptual disability

- dysfunction, as in dyslexic (the reading problem), dysgraphic (the writing problem), dyscalculia (the problem with numbers), and so on
- language disorder
- cognitive defect
- maturational lag
- (minimal) brain dysfunction (we've done that)
- neurophysiological immaturity
- chronic brain syndrome

But speaking of labels, even these have changed — not to protect the innocent, but at least to be a little easier on their damaged egos. I will use the terms *learning disabled* (or l.d.), *perceptually handicapped*, *mentally retarded* (or m.r.), and *brain damaged* almost interchangeably, though there is certainly some difference among these terms. However, I am told that the most acceptable term now is *developmentally handicapped*. This phrase encompasses physical as well as mental handicaps, and covers a very wide range of disability. Times and terms may change; peoples' attitudes don't. We'll get to those.

No matter what you call it, it's a problem. The conditions have existed longer than the words for them, but the conditions are increasing. A recent newspaper article reported that birth defects have doubled in the last twenty-five years. No one knows why they occur. It is suspected that some injuries have chemical causes. Scientists are currently examining the actual brain structure and discovering physical differences between the brains of normally functioning people and those belonging to people identified as brain damaged. Some injuries are accidents of birth; some are caused by a fall or a high fever in infancy. One that I know of was caused by a brief cessation of breathing under anaesthetic during a tonsillectomy (the oxygen supply to the brain was cut off for too long). Everything has been blamed, from acid rain to food additives, from cigarette smoking to the skill of the medical profession in keeping alive infants who used to die. They live now, but damaged in some way.

There are problems and problems. Many learning disabilities are accompanied by other evidences of brain injury, such as epilepsy, cerebral palsy, or deafness. Some children thus afflicted can, nevertheless, possess a normal or an above-normal I.Q., although they are severely hampered by the disability. Brain damage is capricious. No two children are hit the same way. A child can have a very high I.Q. and still have terrible problems because of his dyslexia – the most common and best-known learning disability. It's a reading, no, it's actually a problem in spatial relations, which causes one to flip letters in space. *Dog* becomes *god*, for example, and this is not useful when it comes to reading about Dick and Jane and their dog. If this difficulty is accompanied by a visual memory problem, the kid will have trouble putting letters in their correct order; if he has dysgraphia, he'll have trouble writing the words on paper. Dyscalculia is a similar problem with numbers and number concepts.

Different children are struck in different ways. Though the visual perception problem seems to be the most common, a problem with auditory discrimination may compound the kid's reading difficulties. He will then be unable to sift out, from all the sounds around him, the one he's supposed to be paying attention to. A problem in auditory perception means the child confuses similar sounds (such as *sh* and *ch*, or *g, k, p,* and *b*). And auditory sequential memory defect means he can't remember what he has heard, and therefore has trouble following instructions.

Then there are gross-motor and fine-motor problems. Can he catch a ball? Can he run without falling down? Can he cut paper with scissors? Can he hold a pencil? Can he tie his shoelaces? Can he sit still? How long is his attention span? How is his speech? All these key questions discourage parents when too many of them must be answered in the negative. Imagine how they make the child feel!

Some kids might have only one problem, which should, but doesn't, make things easier since the problem often goes undetected. Girls seem to have fewer problems, but it may only be that they are able to mask them more effectively. Lots of children, male and female, are allowed to slip through school, always dragging at the rear of the class, but nevertheless pushed forward to the next grade, until maybe grade eight or nine. Then someone will do a reading test on them and discover they can barely read at the grade-two level. Where do you start then?

No matter what the actual name of the problem, the fact remains that "twelve per cent of the population up to nineteen years of age, or no less than a million children and youth in Canada today, require attention, treatment and care because of emotional and learning disorders." That's according to the Celdic Report, the 1970 national Commission on Emotional and Learning Disorders in Children. Well, it's one thing to recognize the fact; it's another thing to do something about it. We're still trying to pick the locks and encountering other problems all the way.

So I offer you an account of my son Matthew with the hope that you may learn something from him and from our family life that will help you with yours. Of course, there's pain and anxiety, but there are some happy events, too, and some funny moments. If you don't have a Matthew in your life, you still might want to read this for the story and to find out what one family discovered about children and love. It may also help you to deal with friends and relatives who carry this special burden and blessing with them. If you do have a Matthew, perhaps you will find it possible to learn from a specific case, not in order to generalize, but to particularize, to find applications to your own problems from the solutions applied to someone else's problem. Your child's handicap will change all your lives, as my son's did ours — not only his own life, but my husband's and mine and our other children's and our relationships with each other. It isn't all bad, of course. Over the years I have realized the blessings implicit in the pain and anxiety.

Blesser is a French verb meaning "to wound." In English *bless* means "to confer well-being upon," usually from a divine source (the root of both words means blood). There is a wound in every blessing, and it gives pain while it gives grace. That's one of the incredible paradoxes of life. Remember Jacob wrestling with the angel? In the morning he asked for the angel's blessing, and the angel touched him and he was wounded in the thigh. Perhaps to be blessed is always to receive that wound. You may walk afterwards with a limp but also with the straight, sure carriage of someone who has been truly blessed. I hope you will learn to carry your wound around with you, whatever it is, with pride and humility and pain and love and compassion and gratitude.

CHAPTER TWO

THE BEGINNING

And so it begins. . . .

Hindsight is all very well, but who knew what was going to happen when the doctor put me on amphetamines? We know now—though the doctor never admitted that he considered it to be a possible cause. One of the things we seem to keep learning about the facts of life is how inexorable they are. *After* a fact, you learn to live with it.

Does the beginning of this story begin with my fourth pregnancy, or does it begin earlier when we found out how sick I became during my pregnancies, increasingly so, and how much weight I gained, more with each successive child, at a time when weight gain was not desirable or fashionable? Still, our track record wasn't bad: three perfect babies, two girls and a boy. With the boy, I had discomfort but no troubles. I vomited steadily throughout the pregnancy, forced to eat hourly so the food wouldn't bounce right out again. I gained a lot of weight. At full term I looked like one of those giant Borneo turtles ready to crawl up on a beach to deposit her eggs. But the baby had an easy birth. I was swift and efficient in the delivery and lost nineteen and a half pounds in the process (with only seventeen more to lose!).

John had weighed nine pounds, ten ounces, a big, healthy, strong baby. When the nurse lifted him up to the show window for the proud grandparents to take a look, a friend of my mother's, also a new grandmother, there to admire a tiny baby girl, sniffed at my infant Gargantua and said, "I didn't think they allowed that to happen any more."

My doctor wasn't going to allow it to happen again. Not quite two years later I was pregnant again (we did that in those days) and vomiting daily. He put me on amphetamines, Dexamyl, I think it was. I called it "The Whip." It was supposed to control my excessive weight gain—for what? An easier delivery, a better baby, a slimmer mother? I was prescribed one a day. In those days, those last days before we began to question the wisdom of doctors and the efficacy (and safety) of all drugs, just before the terrible effect of thalidomide was discovered, who was I to argue with my doctor? Docile and obedient, I had my prescription filled.

My father questioned it. He was a doctor and he believed in preserving the divine right of doctors. Even so, when he learned of the prescription, he said, "I have never countermanded another doctor's treatment or prescription. But do me this favour. Instead of taking a pill every day, take one every other day." So I obeyed my father. And survived.

But the every-other-day dosage still had its effects. On the off-days I could sleep. Every other day I could function in the phlegmatic way that I functioned during pregnancy. On the other days, the on-days, I *ran* from morning till night, not only not hungry, but hyper, organized, frenetic, and terribly irritable. My humour ceased, my anxiety level rose with my voice. I shrieked at my other children: one in grade one, two at home with me. I look back at all those children now and wonder what possessed me. We chose to have them—that many and that close together. It was the thing to do. We were part of the pattern of the "big generation." Some of my friends stopped at three. My father said I should have.

"You have both kinds now," he said. "Stop before there's trouble."

I couldn't hear him. I wanted another boy. Then I'd have two of each, a perfect family. Well, we had our boy, but he wasn't perfect. How different our lives might have been if he had been! And how different his life. That's metaphysical though—pure and futile speculation. You take the fact, not the hypothesis, and work with it.

I wasn't very slim, but the foetus was. My doctor asked if I had made a mistake in my dates, because the foetus wasn't the right size according to the original calculations.

A month before I was due, my blood pressure went crazy. Still there was no suggestion that this might be tied in with the amphetamines the doctor thought I was taking daily. And I was so tired! So weary, so tired of being whipped, dragging myself through each day. I had forgotten how to smile.

Oh, but conscientious! The perfect mother. Doing my duty. Cooking up a storm. Planning a birthday party for Kate, stocking up on food and casseroles for the freezer, for the busy time after the baby was born.

Two weeks before the baby was due (it was due on mine and my o.b.'s birthday), I went to see the doctor. I was tired, but I was used to that. My husband picked me up to give me a drive home and waited in the car to take the babysitter home. I sat down on a bench in the front hall — and stayed there. I didn't move. Couldn't, in fact. I sat there in my coat, with my boots on, while the children reported to me. Liz was six and in grade one. Kate was four, going to be five in a week. John was two and a half. Busy ages. They needed a lot of attention. Bill came home and helped me off with my coat.

Somehow I got through dinner. Bill put the children to bed before he went out to curl. I went to bed, too. But the sick, tired feeling never went away, and the contractions began, and my water broke, about 11 P.M., just before Bill came home.

So I went to hospital that night, and Matthew was born the next morning — February 7, 1961.

He was tiny — four and a half pounds. I was briefly unconscious for the moment of delivery. When I came to, they were already working over him. "Is he all right, is he all right, is he all right?" I asked.

Well, he was alive, and so was I, after a nightmare of a night, with tubes plugged into me as if I were a switchboard, and people hovering in a way that tells you all is not well. After the delivery, I was taken back to the labour floor, with my I.V. and plasma and the blood pressure sleeve still hooked up to me. Matthew was wheeled away in an incubator.

We both lived.

Twelve hours later I was put into a private room — a first. The baby was not brought to me. I was given pills to dry up the milk. I cried then.

Bill called the tiny red boy with a mop of beautiful blond hair Big Red. I hadn't seen my baby since he was taken from me in the case room. I was still too weak to walk and he couldn't come to me.

When Big Red had a convulsion in the incubator three days after he was born, we had to give permission for tests to be done to determine the cause. If one of the tests proved positive, the baby would probably die. We are not Roman Catholic but it was important to us that the little red scrap of humanity have a name for God to call him, so we had him baptized: Matthew David — the boy I wanted.

I reread the Book of Job while we waited for the results of the tests.

Matthew didn't die. It turned out that he had been born without any sugar in his blood, and that had caused the convulsion. It also caused some permanent damage to the brain. They hooked him up to a glucose tube and got his blood straightened out. But the damage was done.

It was six months before I was clear. I had a residual high blood pressure that took a while to come down. The moral to that, of course, is don't fool around with drugs when you're pregnant. Who knew?

We know now, with hindsight, and doctors warn pregnant women not to drink alcohol, or smoke tobacco or marijuana, or to take aspirin, or even caffeine. Twenty-four years ago it never occurred to any of us what seems self-evident and obvious now: that whatever the mother-to-be ingests has a direct effect on the foetus. That was just before the thalidomide babies were born.

It seems so impossible now not to have known. And, I must say, if-onlys are hard to live with. Matthew is a bright, humorous, perceptive human being. He'd probably be the brightest of my very bright children — but he has this capricious set of short circuits in his brain that inhibit and impede his learning and his responses. If only I hadn't taken those pills!

Everyone has an if-only to live with at some point in a lifetime. The trick is to accept the fact and go on from there. You can't live your life looking backward. You have to keep moving forward. Every movement forward is progress. I have to believe that.

So there is no blame to be attached. We all stand on the shoulders of giants and each successive generation learns from the preceding one. Now we have trouble believing that people once didn't wash their hands before delivering babies, that doctors went from autopsies to maternity cases with no antisepsis in between. Can we blame people for not knowing something learned by trial and error – the hard way? What we can do is to try to make it possible for others to profit by our mistakes.

I came home alone. Matthew had to stay in the incubator until he reached five pounds and was allowed to leave the hospital. There was plenty for me to do with my three other children, even though the new babe was not with me. I was frightened and tense and still weak. I made a wish for Matthew on my birthday candles, failed to blow them out in one breath, and burst into tears.

Once I was out of the hospital and off the drying pills, my breasts filled up with milk, a painful reminder of the baby I longed to hold. I finally phoned my doctor in agony and begged him to tell me a way to keep my milk until I got the baby. He tried to discourage me but he told me I could rent an electric breast pump and encourage the milk to keep flowing by pumping it out. (It was National Electric Week, my husband joked, and I had breasts a motor could love!)

No one told me I could send the milk to the hospital until about two days before Matthew was discharged. I found out by accident, talking to his day nurse. After that, I sent my milk over for him. At least he got used to the taste.

Our first ordeal was upon us. Little Matt was coming home. I remember I had two special small-size nightgowns made for him, and a tiny flannelette bonnet, because he wouldn't fit the first infant size for at least three months. We brought home a tiny, weak creature to display to the three kids and a contemptuous cleaning lady.

"Mmmff," she sniffed, "he looks like a Dunn-Rite broiler. Don't ask *me* to look after him."

We took a picture of him between two of the girls' dolls. He was the smallest.

You wonder, when you look back, how you got through certain periods of your life. I wonder that a lot when I look back at Matt's life and mine. He weighed five pounds when he finally came home, a mewling kitten of a baby, two weeks old.

The first thing he had to do was learn to nurse. I was told I mustn't fight him, that he was too weak, that if he couldn't or wouldn't nurse, I couldn't do anything but give in. He had to have nourishment. I was told to weigh him before and after every feeding, to see if he took in any food at all. I was told to give him a week, and if he hadn't learned to nurse, to give up and give him a bottle.

I rented baby scales and started. I was accustomed to demand feeding for the first few weeks for my other babies. I thought John had been a challenge. He was so big he was hungry all the time. I nursed him twelve times a day the first few weeks. By six weeks he was down to six feedings a day, the number most babies are on when they come out of hospital. It turned out he was good training for Matthew.

I lost count of how many times a day I nursed Matthew that first week. If he could take in half an ounce of milk and last forty-five minutes to an hour on it, that was terrific. I dropped everything else and concentrated on the baby. It wasn't easy. I had no help. (The mother's help stayed a week, as originally arranged, and moved on.) The other three children needed attention, especially John, who was two and a half and into everything. He got away regularly. I was terrified he was going to run out on the street into the path of a car while I was chained to my chair. I was so grateful if a neighbour offered to take him to the store with her kids. At least I knew he was safe and occupied for an hour.

I dwell on this because it is always the concern for the mother of a child with special needs. You still can't neglect the other children; they have needs, too. It's very difficult not to feel split. The feeling starts very early.

I kept Matthew in our bedroom for the first week so that I could hear his feeble cry in the night. At the end of the week, he had gained weight. He was taking the breast without fighting, and he would sleep two or three hours after a good feeding.

It was his first success and an important one. I later discovered, as I learned about handicapped children, that they become failure-oriented very quickly. That first learning of Matthew's, though he might not consciously remember it, was of enormous importance to him psychologically. He had overcome his first problem.

Not that it was all easy after that. He was still small. He wasn't up to an average baby's birth weight until he was over three months old, and he still took a lot of time, time the other children didn't get from me.

How can I give it to them now, or ask their forgiveness for my constant anxiety, weariness, and irritation? It's one of the problems parents are constantly aware of, from the very beginning, when they have a handicapped child. Time becomes unbalanced and so do priorities. Each child is entitled to an equal share of your love and care. Some shares become more equal than others, though. Your intentions are good, you know that, but where is the time?

My husband was wonderful. He was emotionally supportive of me, and he did what he could on weekends. But the children were always my job. If there were special problems I couldn't solve, I would ask for his help and advice. But it was my task to define and evaluate the problem first.

Parents today frequently share more of the parenting, or say they do. Parents today also have more divorces, and then mothers, usually, are left with *all* the parenting. The incidence of divorce among parents with handicapped children is high. I'm not trying to draw any hard conclusions from these statements. I'm talking about priorities. It's difficult but necessary to come to terms as quickly as you can with what you can hope to achieve with your handicapped child. Then, if you can, set your priorities and stick with them. The child, ideally, can become another binding force in your lives rather than a divisive one.

It helps to share your burden and your anxiety with your mate rather than shutting him or her out. You are not the only one with disappointed expectations, blunted hopes, and extra financial pressures because of this child. Tackle the problems together, but don't let them colour all your time together.

And so with the other children. If you can, make it clear to them that though this child takes more of your time, he does not necessarily take more of your love. I'm not sure that I managed to do that, make it clear, I mean. I tried, and I learned as I went along.

Just don't take anything for granted. All you can do is to try to cope with each day's problems as they arise. Don't lose faith in your own ability. "Mother knows best." It's a phrase you don't often hear any more. But it still has some truth in it. Trust your own instincts. And don't let go of your own life. That's one of the chief dangers that face a couple with a problem child. The rest of the relationship suffers because both husband and wife are so busy worrying about the baby. If there are other children in the family as well, watch them.

Easier said than done, and I'll be the first one to admit that. You're human, after all, and you're struggling with situations you've never thought of, let alone faced before. Try to reserve some time for yourself, enough time to keep your perspective, your sense of humour, your love, and your generosity intact.

So talk more, laugh more, repeat more, do more, play more, love more. Whether or not your child has a problem, and it may be too soon to tell, what you're doing won't hurt and it might help (like chicken soup).

Here's another tough one, a task you have to keep setting yourself and coming back to many, many times in the course of your life. Try to come to terms with your own hopes and expectations for your child as soon as you can. Many devoted parents, mothers especially, set out to seek a "cure." Cures don't exist. Once damage has been done, you live with it, cope with it, compensate for it, get around it, make it part of the given in any situation. But there are no miracle cures.

In *A Day in the Death of Joe Egg*, a play by Peter Nichols about a child, "a kind of living parsnip," and her effect on her parents' relationship, the mother fantasizes what it would be like if the child were normal. Up to this scene, the child has been in a carriage, wheeled about and talked at, completely passive. Suddenly, with a change of lights, she dances onto the stage and whirls about, everyone's image of perfection in childhood, and the mother's dream for her Joe Egg. Life just doesn't work that way. You can hurt yourself and your child if you hold this impossible dream too tightly. Learn to accept and love your child for what he/she is. Help, teach, encourage, demand certainly, but take pride in lesser achievements than you might have hoped for. They might be lesser to you; they are Everests of accomplishment to your child.

Every child needs stimulus; l.d. (learning-disabled) and m.r. (mentally retarded) kids need more. They don't learn by osmosis; everything they learn, they learn the hard way. But every child *can* learn and never stops learning. It just takes longer for some, and it's harder.

Life's difficulties, from which no one is exempt, present more stress to a child who has a central problem. Death or divorce in the family can be doubly traumatic to someone whose inner resources are shaky at best. Such an event adds to the already existing feelings of inadequacy and reinforces the knowledge that he is not normal. Matthew's father died when Matt was twelve years old, a difficult time in any boy's life, doubly difficult for him. Be aware, as we had to learn to be, that even while you're coping with special needs, the daily blows that life deals also have to be met—with guts and grace.

What you hope for is a functioning human being. Some people can't even hope for that. You want space in society for this human being to live in dignity and without fear, shame, degradation, or exploitation. That's what we all need and want. If some of us can manage to do more, that's a bonus, icing on the cake. Each of us has to learn that before we can teach it to anyone else. Your child is going to teach you, just as Matthew taught us.

CHAPTER THREE

THE LEARNING PROCESS

Educators are still fascinated and baffled by the act of learning. As I write this, they're exploring the possibility of computers taking over all the skills of the human brain. The exploration is uncovering more and more skills, unknown responses, and abilities in the human brain than anyone had thought of. Learning, of course, is one of the most dazzling and incomprehensible feats. When you come right down to it, how does anyone learn anything?

Never underestimate the power of the human brain. We all function normally at about 30 per cent of our total brain capacity. When one portion of the brain is damaged, it is often possible to open up a new area. People who have suffered strokes do this and relearn a vocabulary or some lost skill. So with a brain-damaged child: although some of the involuntary processes have not been programmed into his faulty computer, it is possible to open up new circuits and help him learn what other children learn naturally, effortlessly, and normally.

You take the whole process for granted until you have a learning-disabled child. Then the lapses and the short circuits evident in his learning process make you realize the incredible feats human beings, especially very young human beings, perform in their preparation for life.

Learning, according to the dictionary, is the act of acquiring some knowledge or skill. It's a process, actually. It doesn't happen all at once or all of a piece in any human being. Our lives are full of revelations; we go on learning useful information, acquiring new skills and techniques, understanding new concepts and old truths, as long as we live—if we're lucky. Some people stop learning and atrophy, but I'm not thinking about them. I'm thinking about the ones who keep on finding difficulties, who never completely master skills that others take for granted from the time they're six years old.

The learning process. Oh, my, yes! We do take it for granted with normal children. One weekend, when Kate was about a year and a half, I tried to write down all the words she knew. Her vocabulary that weekend alone increased by about thirty words a day. I couldn't keep up with her.

Early on, Liz had shown an aptitude for colour. She was only about two when I was colouring a picture with her and chose a tan-coloured crayon to colour a chicken. For a couple of days she called that colour "chicken" and picked it out easily from the box of forty-eight crayons.

One Sunday morning when we were still asleep, three-year-old John got out of bed, took all the liquid shoe polish, both red and white, from the bathroom cupboard and carefully filled every possible container in the living room with it, neither mixing colours nor spilling a drop. (He also didn't drink any of it, thank goodness.)

Matthew would exhibit none of these feats. Still, his achievements were very real.

Just think how complicated learning really is. It involves:

1) skill—the ability to perform a task,
2) content—the ability to recall information,
3) concepts—the ability to understand an idea.

It's a wonder most of us are walking around, functioning, keeping ourselves clean and presentable, going about our duties, earning our living, paying our bills, driving our cars, playing our pianos or guitars, and laughing at each other's jokes. How did we ever manage all that? And we each have lapses we'd rather not admit: some strange inability to keep track of our belongings (don't you know people who leave a trail behind them?), some awkwardness in connecting a bat with a ball or a racquet with a bird, some inexplicable blank when it comes to remembering names, some geographical illiteracy, some mathematical weakness, some trouble reading a clock. Not all things come easily even to so-called "normal" people. Yet we learned. Somehow we passed grade four, most of us. It's a wonder, because our mothers probably wondered whether we'd ever learn enough to come in out of the rain. Parents of l.d. kids wonder the same thing, and a lot more.

Matthew was still not sitting up by the time he was eleven months old. (John walked at nine months.) He was a healthy baby, thanks to the breast-milk, I think (I weaned him at seven months), but he was still small and lean and not very strong. He didn't crawl on his hands and knees; he dragged himself along on his stomach pulling himself with his forearms. The front of all his clothes got very dirty as he acted as a mop on my floors.

I have since read of an exercise called cross-patterning, which some experts think contributes to a child's reading ability, or at least prepares him to read. Children who never crawl, the theory goes, have not developed the balance between the right and left hemispheres of their brains and so will have trouble reading across a page of print. I have read of teams of neighbours and friends coming in to help parents cross-pattern a child, spending hours pulling right knee and left hand forward, and then left knee and right hand. If your child is young enough and if you think it will help, you can get down on your hands and knees and race with him, play games with him, play hide-and-seek, whatever.

But I hadn't heard of cross-patterning then. Our pediatrician sent us to a doctor who had taken his M.D. at the University of Manitoba Medical School, and who had just completed his postgraduate studies in Boston, specializing in child development. He had set up a new department at the children's hospital in Winnipeg. Matthew was one among this man's first thirty-two patients who were slow in their development. This was in 1962, a year before the Association for Children with Learning Disabilities (ACLD) was formed in Toronto. Matthew was a pioneer.

At eleven months, as I said, he was not sitting up. I used to stuff a foam pillow around him in his feeding table so that he could sit to be fed, and he could manage to hold himself fairly upright in his jumper chair. But he was happy lying on his back in the playpen playing with things with his hands and feet. When he wanted to go somewhere he pulled himself around on his stomach.

Matthew had no fine-motor control at all. He grasped at objects with his whole fist rather than with his fingers, and he couldn't balance one block on top of another.

Of course, I knew he wasn't progressing the way the others had, but it was painful, nevertheless, to watch him struggle through those first tests with the doctor. With all your children you want to pave the way for them, make it (whatever it is) easier for them than it was for you. Even more so with a child who just doesn't quite make it. You want to do it for him.

I think I learned then not to be a comparison shopper with my children. Each child is a separate creation, a total individual unto his- or herself, and must be related to, dealt with, trained, helped, and loved according to his/her own needs and strengths. That's important to remember, I guess, when you have any child, let alone a handicapped one.

The major problems had to be dealt with first. His big muscles were not ready to enable Matthew to sit, stand, or walk, so we had to concentrate on those first. I was taught a series of exercises to do with him twice daily to strengthen his stomach muscles so that he would be able to sit.

These exercises were really sit-ups for babies. I grasped his hands, but gradually changed so that he was grasping my fingers, and gently pulled him up from a prone to a sitting position, then just as gently let him down again. All this was done as a game with a lot of talking and encouragement. It was only an extra hour a day.

I don't know about Matthew, because he didn't tell me, but my stomach and arm muscles were really stiff the first week we started the exercises. But they worked — miraculously. Within a few weeks Matthew could sit without support and without toppling sideways. A few weeks after that he could get himself up into a sitting position. All it took was time.

"This child," I was told, "will need more attention and more direct, focused stimulus than any of your children. You can't take his learning process for granted. Everything has to be spelled out for him." This statement continues to be true for a learning-disabled person for his entire life. The stimuli have to be in strong contrast to what is going on, so that they engage his attention. They have to be repeated regularly, so as to ensure his memory of them. And they can only be effective when he is ready for them.

With a normal child, given normal stimuli, auto-education takes over. Attention is followed by observation, observation by action — that is, by the absorption of the stimulus into his range of understanding. Tests follow, and in the case of mistaken or unsuccessful application, further processing of the information goes on. Errors are then eliminated or controlled. Ever watched a very young child pour a glass of milk?

Which brings us to the next, frequently accompanying problem in an l.d. child — coordination. The hand and eye seem to function independently of each other; one can never be sure if the hand knows what it's doing. Liz says she still remembers watching Matt attempt to butter his own toast for the first time and *aching* to do it for him. But she contained herself and let him do it. It's called patience, and that's one of the most important keys to the learning process in an l.d. child. Patience, and its corollary, repetition.

Stimulus, patience, repetition, reinforcement — and don't take anything for granted. I guess that's called cynicism, but it's coupled with humility and gratitude for your own blessings and respect for this other human being you're trying to equip for life. Those are the tools of any educator; they must be in excellent condition when one is trying to teach someone who is learning disabled.

So we gave Matthew exercises to teach him to sit, then to stand, then to walk. It was slow, but he learned. He is still learning; he hasn't stopped. None of us does. We keep on learning, or we do if we're lucky, until we're too sick or old or feeble to continue. In Matthew's case, we simply trained new areas of his brain to learn and then to take over for the damaged parts and function automatically in the performance of his necessary skills.

I would put his feet on my midriff and lean on him, forcing his legs to bend while he pushed back. He was gaining strength. I could tell, because I was so stiff. I bicycled his legs until my arms ached. Only an extra half hour, twice a day.

On and on we went. He sat up. He stood up. He walked. Everyone took turns holding his fingers while he tottered about. We were all so proud of him. Never again would I take a child's achievements lightly.

Well, those were the lessons I was taught to do with Matthew. I started inventing my own as well.

His fine-motor control—that is, his ability to grasp small objects—was abysmal. I invented a game. When he was sitting in his feeding table keeping me company in the kitchen while I cooked, I would sprinkle some sugared cereal or raisins on the surface in front of him, just a few at a time. He started trying to pick them up and put them in his mouth. Gradually, he learned to control his fingers and to use his wonderful opposable thumb to pick up one raisin.

All it takes is time.

All my life I have prayed for patience. My mother told me when I was very young that I was an impatient child, impossible to live with. That's when I began to pray, "Teach me to be patient, Lord." So the Lord sent me Matthew, to teach me patience. My kids will argue that I still have some more to learn, but they didn't know me when I was younger.

In the meantime, Matthew's face and personality were a beauty and a joy. I had trouble getting rid of babysitters because they stood at the door and raved about this beautiful child with the angelic smile. He was totally surrounded with love and care and approval and support, and he responded like a hothouse flower to all that warmth and nurturing. That's one of the secrets of raising any child and I wish I had learned it earlier: total acceptance, love, approval. Certainly, one can be demanding, expecting this small creature to learn to function independently and to learn life skills. That is the goal for each of us. But there are ways and ways of teaching. Inexorable love is the best way, I think. If at first you don't succeed, try, try again—especially if the child you're working with is handicapped.

Perhaps you will find, as I did, that you have an overwhelming sense of responsibility. It must be a common burden. I felt that the baby's progress was totally my responsibility, that a day on which I neglected to take him through his exercises, or failed to teach him something, was a lost day, never to be recovered. I always had this sense of urgency. In a way it was justified. I was the only person who really knew what to do with and for him. He did need constant stimulation and encouragement. I kept discovering new areas of activity I had to initiate for him — to the neglect of the other children and of projects of my own (I wanted to be a writer.) It may sound as if I had an overdeveloped sense of duty, but I was constantly and sharply reminded of that duty when I failed to do it.

Unless someone was watching him constantly, Matthew was safer in a playpen. He couldn't sit up comfortably for a long time, so he would lie in his playpen and run a baby Busy Box with his feet. My memory now is of him lying in the playpen for hours, just behind my back. I was at the typewriter in the afternoons while the girls were at school and John was out exploring with a friend. I kept trying to write in my "spare time."

It was about that time that Matthew developed a new habit. After I put him in his crib at night, he would bounce, rock up and down, and pound his buttocks on the mattress. This would go on for fifteen minutes to half an hour before he went to sleep. I consulted with the doctor. Matt wasn't getting enough exercise or stimulus during the day. The bouncing made him tired enough to go to sleep. You see? If I failed him in some way, there were consequences.

Maybe I was wrong to try to do it all by myself. And yet my husband was busy, and if I had to choose between his spending time with me or time with the baby, I wanted his time with me. My children were young; I couldn't saddle them with too much of a burden. Years later, on a television show, Liz commented that she and her brother and sister never felt that they were forced to help. Matt never became a burden to them, she said. No one made her feel guilty about not helping him or held her back to wait for him. That's how she felt, anyway. So maybe that was a good thing. You do what you can. You do what you feel you have to do.

"Does he make his wants known?" the doctor asked, early on in those gruelling assessment meetings. Yes, oh, yes! Matthew had an acute sense of his own needs. Though he was a long time speaking he could point and growl and grunt and mime to get what he wanted. He was a veritable Gerald McBoing-Boing, with a whole range and vocabulary of sounds that helped him to make his wants known.

Even so, I set about creating an environment that met his wants, at once structured and stimulating. With a normal child you can play around with meal- and bedtimes (though I don't think it does anyone much good), but with a special child you have to set up the daily living patterns so that the child learns to trust them and learn them, too. You can't take anything for granted with a handicapped child. However simple an idea, a lesson, or task may seem to you, you cannot assume that it will be understood or assimilated automatically by the child merely upon presentation or demonstration. You have to spell it out. Bring it to his attention. Notice it — out loud. State why such-and-such a thing is important or useful or interesting or necessary — and keep on saying it until you're sure he knows it. Remind him later.

I guess the structure was good for all of us. It centred us all, gave us a continuing and demanding focus. By the time my husband was in the theatre business and we were into the different rhythms of life that that involved, we still carried our structured centre with us. If we had had four normal children, we would probably have left them to fend for themselves more. As it was, we kept the family's structure and routine as unchanged as possible, for Matthew's sake.

So how do you structure an environment? I guess it really centres around the table. If mealtime is patterned and structured, everything else falls into place. I remember when we were driving across the country to attend Expo 67 (it's a wonder Canada didn't tip that year and slide us all into the Atlantic Ocean). Our first day on the road, towards the end of the day, Matthew, by that time age six, began to get very nervous.

It was about 4 P.M. and we had been driving all day, stopping for a picnic lunch. He knew we hadn't turned back. He started asking about dinner and bedtime. How far was it to his bed? Where were we going to eat? We tried to explain, but the best explanation was a demonstration. We stopped driving, found a motel with a swimming pool, had a swim, ate dinner, spent the night, and the next day started driving again. At 4 P.M. that day, Matthew asked, "Swim now? Going to have supper? Sleep?" He had caught on to the new routine, so that's what he expected.

That's the best illustration I can give. The routine sets up expectations, and when they are fulfilled, daily, they somehow create a feeling of security in the child.

Perhaps it was easier for me to accomplish the routine because I already had three children and I was used to it. If a special child is a couple's first child, it must be more difficult because one has a double adjustment to make: to the child and to the handicap.

Once a recognizable structure is in place, it becomes easier to verbalize any changes and to give advance warning of them. Then a trip, such as the one we took to Quebec, becomes a pleasure and not a battle of wills.

Some learning-disabled children are what is called hyperactive – they never stop moving, talking, teasing, jiggling, arguing, and tearing around. Structure helps them a lot, too. A routine they can count on, a quiet place as well as a place to let off steam, these are what their families can provide. Outings tend to get them too excited, and yet you don't want to deny them enjoyable experiences.

I remember, after we had moved to Stratford, we took the whole family to a matinee performance of *The Three Musketeers*. You know the story, about D'Artagnan and his three fencing buddies. It's very exciting. After Matt came home from the show, he sat on the floor of his bedroom and yelled for half an hour. And he's never been classified as hyperactive!

The point is that you have to be careful with stimulation, too. Too little, and the child will never learn anything. Too much, and he'll blow a circuit. It helps if you can be subtle about your control over possibly stressful situations. There's a funny rule to the effect that no matter what time you have decided to leave a party, a child's tears always start five minutes before. You learn to keep a weather eye on your child. Also on other parents.

There was a little boy Matthew liked to play with. I used to worry about it, however, because he always came home scarlet-faced and far too wound up. The mother didn't care what the kids did and never put a stop to anything, whether it was a pillow- or a fist-fight or jumping off the end of the living-room sofa. Some of you are going to think I'm a fussy mother, and you're absolutely right. But the structure worked for us. I'm not saying you have to be a prison warden or anything like that. Structure simplifies your own life, too, because you don't have to make new decisions constantly. And it's perfectly possible to include other people in your plans – when you have plans.

There is a school of thought that has gained some credence that says that junk foods and foods with chemical additives contribute to hyperactivity in some young people. Tests have been and are still being conducted and are definitive or inconclusive depending on which report you read. If you want to investigate further, go ahead. It never hurt anyone to eat more natural foods.

All these fads and ideas—cross-patterning, chemicals in foods, structuring—and many more have been introduced and considered since Matthew was born. Like every anxious mother seeking a "cure" I read voraciously, searching out experts and methods to help Matt with his problems. I read Montessori books, I read Jean Piaget's theories of education, I read about the Summerhill school, I read Glenn Doman's book *How to Teach Your Baby to Read*, and I haunted educational toy stores. I never stopped searching, trying to find ways to help Matthew "catch up."

And all the time the gap was widening.

CHAPTER FOUR

THERAPY

Therapy comes from the Greek, meaning "healing." Strictly speaking, therapy still means healing; it is, according to my dictionary, medical treatment of a disease. But we mean much more when we speak of therapy, especially in the case of a brain-injured child. Therapy becomes every single activity by which he might learn or improve some skill, develop some muscle, practise some lesson – anything that he needs to keep on becoming more "normal," more acceptable, more adaptive, more able to live in this world. There isn't anything that happens during the day that doesn't become a learning opportunity. Therapy becomes a way of life.

Therapy begins at home and touches everything a human being must be able to do in order to survive and to function in society. As a parent and guide of a brain-injured child, you become an opportunist, capitalizing on everything that happens during the day. If you think this makes a mother (or a father) a nudge and a nag, you're wrong. The whole process of learning is endlessly fascinating. You mustn't assume anything; you learn not to take anything for granted. When you have a handicapped child you learn to make each moment count. Taking the time to make each moment of the day meaningful makes each moment more precious.

Matthew would run down the corridor laughing and charge into the occupational therapist's office at the children's hospital in Winnipeg. He was four years old and he had made his first conquest – no, there were all those babysitters who fell in love with him before that.

We went once a month to the O.T. to learn new exercises and show his progress. We were doing gross-motor therapy and also starting on more finely tuned hand-eye work. By this time, obviously, he had learned to sit, stand, walk, and run. But if he had to pick his way over the snaking cord of a vacuum cleaner he would get tangled in his own feet and fall down, and he tended to go upstairs with two feet on each step, and on tiptoe. We had to do something about his heel tendons so he wouldn't walk on his toes for the rest of his life.

At his age everything had to be a game. The therapist showed me how to build a tower of blocks beside Matt's foot—inside or outside. Then I had to hold his leg rigid, pressing firmly on his knee, and encourage him to knock down the tower by moving his foot right or left depending on where the tower was.

John liked this game, too, and he was very good at it. I tried to include him in the games when I could. I can remember him sitting on the top level of the boys' bunk beds, watching me play with Matt, wanting so much to play, too, wanting me to give him that kind of attention. It was a dilemma I couldn't solve. Sometimes Bill would take him away and read to him. That helped. And I lengthened Matthew's afternoon therapy session to do the things that absolutely required one-on-one work.

For example, I'd sit cross-legged on the floor with Matt in my lap and my arms around him so that I could guide each hand with mine. Then we would take paper in one hand and scissors in the other and slowly, awkwardly we would start. "Open them, shut them, open them, shut them," I'd say, and Matt would parrot me and try to make his scissors hand open and shut so that the scissors would cut the paper.

Everything we did had to be verbalized to help him with his speech. It was not enough merely to do it, he had to know what he was doing, and be able to express it. I collected a bunch of things in a paper bag and I would sit behind him and hand him one thing at a time. He had to feel the object behind his back and then tell me what it was—a curl of dust from under the bed, a ball of cat fluff, a cotton ball, a piece of silk, a piece of terry towel, a piece of sandpaper, a piece of writing paper, some dried-up chewing gum, a pebble. I kept trying to think of things to put in that bag. The trick was not only to identify the object but to describe its property: rough, smooth, soft, and so on. John liked that one, too.

An educational toy I bought had a collection of shapes — a crescent, rectangle, square, circle — that had to be fitted into the appropriate holes in a tray. When Matthew became proficient at that, I made him do it behind his back. I'd hand him the shape; he'd feel it and point to the hole it would fit before he looked at it.

I took him through the Frostig Program. Dr. Marianne Frostig, one of the better-known workers with brain-injured children in the United States, has developed an entire program in visual perception (published by Follett Publishing in Chicago). It's a huge series of exercises in various aspects of visual perception: figure ground, spatial relations (i.e., left-right, beside-behind, above-below concepts), and so on. Each of these exercises ultimately is designed to prepare an injured brain to cope with learning how to read. The exercises consist of a series of pictures with a problem in each one. The problem might be as simple as getting from Point A to Point B by drawing a line within a prescribed path from one side (the left side) of the paper to the other. But the path in succeeding exercises grows increasingly circuitous, and the child must guide his stylus carefully (I used felt pens) so as not to go outside the path.

Matthew liked Batman and Robin so I told him Batman and Robin stories as I drew the exercises for him on big sheets of newsprint. (I bought huge pads of newsprint at a craft store.)

"Here's Batman," I'd say, drawing Batman on the right side of the page, "and he's about to be boiled in oil," and I'd draw a tub of oil that poor Batman was about to be lowered into. "And here's Robin," I'd say, drawing Robin on the left side of the page, "and he's going to rescue Batman." Then I'd draw a double-lined path for Matt to follow with his felt pen, taking Robin to save Batman. The path was straight at first, but gradually more and more loops and switchbacks were added until Robin was flying all over the page to save his buddy. Matt loved the game and never tired of it. The therapist would lend me sheets with the exercises on them, and I would reproduce them and numerous variations of them on my newsprint. Matt's hand-eye coordination improved enormously. But that was a simple one.

Figure ground was more difficult, and harder for me to draw, too. I would draw the outline of a doll or a car or some other shape, and then draw other lines all over the page in and around and over the figure that Matt had to outline with his felt pen. This exercise grew more and more difficult depending on the number of figures in it that he had to outline. It took a lot of drawing.

One of the most difficult concepts for Matthew to understand was the relationship of objects to each other — that is, spatial relations. The basic exercises consisted of three or four sets of objects on the left-hand side of the page, paralleled by three or four sets on the other side. A square might be depicted in front of a circle, then a square beside a circle, then a square behind a circle. On the other side, there would be a triangle behind a circle, then a triangle in front of a circle, then a triangle beside a circle. Matt had to draw a line between the relationships that were the same. He had real trouble (I think he still does).

Up, over, behind, beside, above, below, and so on are difficult ideas to picture in one's mind. I can't do a flip in my mind of any route I take in the car. I mean, I can't reverse my tracks and go back the way I came. I get hopelessly lost unless I get new instructions when I leave. I have to admit I also get lost in hotel corridors; I always turn the wrong direction when I get out of the elevator. I'm sure it's a form of brain damage. So I can appreciate how difficult these ideas are to learn and internalize.

Once I lost my patience. We were trying to do an exercise such as the one I described, illustrating the beside, behind, in-front-of concepts, and Matt simply could not understand it. I started to raise my voice; he got tense and locked in. I ended the session and went for a walk. One mustn't get too tense, or the purpose is defeated. There has to be a lot of success and a lot of fun or it's no use at all. Usually we had both, but this one day the concept was simply not getting through. When that happens, it's best not to dwell on it or try to fight or shout it through. The child only gets nervous and can't function as well. I know I don't like being yelled at. I always do better work if I'm encouraged. Why shouldn't a brain-injured child feel the same way?

Sometimes, if a child is feeling particularly harassed, he will fall into a behaviour pattern called perseveration. He will keep on saying or doing the same thing even though he knows it's wrong.

It's as if his mind has fallen into a track—or rut—that he can't get out of. The closest thing like that to help a "normie" understand this frustrating behaviour (as frustrating to the child as it is to the teacher or parent) is to remind you of some days when you can't get a tune out of your head. Every spare minute, you find the same melody, more likely one line of it, running over and over again in your head, like a record that's stuck. That's a form of perseveration. The only way to get away from it is to get away from it. Walk away.

So I walked away. That's all you can do. There's no sense sitting there and screaming. That's no good for either of you. I have since read that some parents can't work with their brain-injured child because all their sessions end up in frustration and rage. If that happens to you, then walk away. Don't worry about it.

Oddly enough, a few weeks later, when I returned to that exercise, Matt was able to do it. Was that a breakthrough, or simply development?

I do sometimes wonder now how much good all that effort accomplished, other than a very close relationship with my son. When we moved to Stratford, our first contact with a diagnostic specialist was a doctor in Toronto. Dutifully I took our work sheets in to show him as I had been doing with our O.T. in Winnipeg. The doctor dismissed them with an airy wave of his hand. "He would have done as well with normal progress," he said. I was indignant. But would he have?

There's always that uncertainty. There are so many experts to tell parents what they're doing wrong, and so many problems in the child that are blamed on parents (and if you haven't had that happen, you will). Before any serious diagnosis of your child, someone is bound to say that his problems are the parents' fault. Easier to blame a neurotic mother than discover the cause.

But was what the doctor said true? Were all those good things I did with Matthew wasted? Years later, the principal of the special school Matt was attending told me she and her staff were doing things that I had done with Matt in those early early days. She assumed that he had never had these things taught to him before. He had, but he had forgotten. Was all that effort wasted?

No energy, it is said, is wasted. I have to believe that. All that work with Matthew probably made me feel better. At least I was doing something about his problems.

The point is that you keep on trying. You want your child to do as well as he can. You want to help him. So you do all these things, spend all this time and money and effort, and you wonder if it does any good. All I can say is, keep on trying. But ... make it fun. Try not to lose your perspective. Remember there are no "cures." Don't push too hard. Relax. Enjoy. Make sure your child knows you prize him and love him whether or not he can draw a line from Point A to Point B. Tell him you love him and praise him when he does well.

But remember that it is possible to go overboard on praise. Genuine achievement is one thing, and the child himself usually knows when he has done something special, that is, for him, or something he has never been able to do before. But he knows when anyone overdoes the praise and he knows when it is undeserved — or he should, if parents and well-meaning relatives don't distort his perception of his own achievements. Insincere praise is flattery in any context and doesn't do an l.d. child any good. Better to save praise for something that deserves it.

Even the tone of the praise should be watched. A good, firm comment — "Good work, Matt" — is better than an overblown aria — "Oh, my, did you do that all by yourself? Imagine that!" Kids know.

Just as bad as excessive praise is reverse discrimination, giving special favours to a special child because life has short-changed him. Life doesn't work like that. If anything, life is harder on handicapped people than on those who are not. No quarter is given; no quarter should be expected. Certainly, you have to give the child the tools to survive: extra time, extra equipment. But he must learn to cope by himself. Ain't no one going to do him no favours once he's out in the cold, cruel world. So don't give him, and don't let doting relatives give him the idea that he is very good at something he's not very good at, or that he can get away with sloppy work or undisciplined behaviour because he's special and therefore somehow exempt from life's rules. He's not, and it handicaps him even further if he thinks he is.

All the funny little therapy tips I'm going to tell you about now may seem to have no relevance to you and your child's situation. But each child is so unique and the brain is so diverse, even in damage, that there may be something in this apparent hodgepodge that you can use. You never know when and where you might find something useful, so you keep looking. That's what I did, all those years, picking up ideas, activities, games, lessons, routines, equipment; whatever I could find to fill in all those gaps in my son's learning.

Can your child tie his shoelaces? Matthew couldn't, not for years. By the time he was in school I thought I had solved the social problem accompanying this inability by dressing him in loafers — pull-on shoes with no laces. But then I discovered that they didn't give enough support to his growing feet so he had to go back to shoes with laces. Long-suffering teachers, patient friends, and not-so-patient siblings helped him by tying his shoelaces for him. Meanwhile, he practised at home. That's therapy. (There are running shoes available now with Velcro fasteners.)

Does your child have difficulty dressing himself? I used to lay out the clothes like an empty scarecrow on the floor in the order that Matt was to put them on, and right-side-up (of course). Then all I had to do was give him plenty of time. If you do this, keep in mind that it helps to sew buttons on with elastic thread. A little more give in the thread will resist those desperate, uncoordinated fingers. It also helps to buy good quality cotton T-shirts because they don't get pulled out of shape so quickly by flailing arms and obdurate shoulders.

Zippers and flies were a problem. For years after he should have been, Matt was pulling his pants down to pee. It was easier for him than to cope with the fly in his pants and underwear. Heaven knows what kind of persecution he went through in the boys' bathroom. I was afraid to ask. I did notice, though, that he often came home in a terrible rush to get to the bathroom. Learning to work zippers is therapy. Keep old ones to practise on.

Velcro was a godsend. I bought winter boots with Velcro fastenings and found snowsuits (two-piece) with Velcro closings. I also found dry-cleaners who would replace zippers on jackets. That's a kind of therapy, too. You have to learn to be a careful shopper, to find clothes that your child will find relatively easy to put on and take off, and find ways to fix things that don't last as long as they were intended to with normal use.

What else?

From the time he was about two years old, Matthew took swimming lessons. It was years, of course, before he could swim (John swam his first length when he was four), but he learned to be confident in the water and he enjoyed "swimming" with the family. I used to strap him into a vest-type life-jacket the moment we stepped onto the dock at our place in the Whiteshell in Manitoba. He "walked" in the water. Every day he would swim across the bay with me, sort of bicycling his legs as he bobbed upright in the lake. It did wonders for his leg muscles. Since I was a good swimmer, I would sometimes remove his life-jacket and give him a ride on my back, like a mama whale. He learned to hold lightly onto my shoulders and I would swim breast stroke, head up. Then, within a few feet of a dock, I would shake him off, and he would swim the rest of the way by himself. I could even take him out to a diving platform like that. That's therapy.

Does your child walk curbs? Do you remember walking curbs when you were a kid? There's another theory that if a child doesn't walk curbs or fences, he won't learn to read as easily. It has something to do with right-left hemisphere balance. We bought a long two-by-four and balanced it on two bricks in the basement for Matt to "walk the plank." Then we played pirate, but often we had to hold the pirate's hand, to help him keep his balance as he walked.

How is his balance? I cut out big circles from construction paper (I haunted craft stores) and set them out on the basement floor to create stepping stones for Matt to walk on — another aid to right-left balance. More fun to go to Aunt Sally's farm, though, as a family. The "farm" was at Assiniboine Park in Winnipeg with real live farm animals for kids to see and pat. (A cow is as rare to a city child these days as an ostrich.) There was a pond in the farm with big concrete stepping-stones for one to cross it. Guess who slipped off a stepping-stone and put her foot into the water. Liz, the oldest!

Is there a split between the right and left hemispheres of your child's brain? How would you know? Apparently brain-injured people have difficulty drawing a line across the front of their bodies. If asked to draw a straight line across the board, they will draw it from the left side to the centre of the board and then either lift the chalk and continue from a new starting point, or shift their position so that they are no longer centred in the middle of the line. Bill found an enormous square piece of greenboard (it was so much easier when they were called blackboards) for Matt to draw on. (It also went into the basement.) So we practised drawing lines. All, all in the name of therapy.

Does your child express himself well? Can he talk? (Does he make his wants known?) I bought talking toys. Do you remember Chatty Cathy and her friends? I used to pull the string on Matt's talking Bugs Bunny and answer it, no matter what it said, in what order — sometimes it repeated a lot. I would pretend to get angry at it for nagging me when it repeated itself and I talked non-stop back at it. Matt would go into paroxysms of laughter at this. There is a talking dog now; it doesn't say as much as our voluble Bugs Bunny, but it does communicate, and that's what you want your child to do. There are records you can put on your Fisher-Price record-player. The funniest talking toy I ever saw was a talking telephone Matt's speech therapist tried out on him. Different records carried on different conversations, my favourite being a New York deli clerk offering the specials for the day. Speak & Spell and the teaching toy with sound effects (oink, oink) and voice ("This is a pig") aren't nearly as much fun. Still, they're worth trying.

Learning-disabled kids frequently have speech problems: if not actual physical problems, then ones caused by their inability to organize and communicate their thoughts. So any efforts you make involving speech and expression are good therapy. Puppets are useful, too.

Judy Ball came into Matt's life because his orthodontist had ordered tongue therapy. Nothing in the kid's life was ever simple. In the first place, there was no orthodontist in Stratford, so we had to drive to London, Ontario. In the second place, the dentist couldn't start work until Matt rearranged his tongue. Seems he had a reverse tongue thrust.

Go ahead. Swallow right now. Your tongue probably (at least it should) goes up and back. Matt's went down and out, thus pushing his teeth around and messing up his saliva and speech. So we went to a speech therapist to work on his tongue. Another blessing in disguise. Judy Ball became another of Matt's mentors and helpers. When she moved from the Crippled Children's Centre over to the

Children's Psychiatrist Research Institute to start a speech-therapy clinic there, she spirited Matt with her and kept on giving him speech therapy and language lessons long after the tongue exercises were over. She and her husband left London about the same time that we left Stratford, but we have kept in touch.

One of the first things Judy Ball gave Matt was an auditory-discrimination program to work through, via tapes.

Enter the tape recorder. As part of his talking toy arsenal, Matt had a small, inexpensive tape recorder but I hadn't been using it for therapy as such. He used to love to make soundtracks. He would record noises into his tape recorder—screaming, yelling, shouting, strangling, gagging, gargling, groaning, moaning, dying—for hours on end or until the tape ended, whichever came first. Then he would stuff coats and jackets with towels and strew them about the floor, preferably the basement recreation-room floor. He would turn out all the lights and come upstairs and invite whoever was around, preferably unsuspecting guests, to come and see his haunted house. The guests would carefully pick their way down the stairs accompanied by bloodcurdling screams and piteous moans to trip over the "bodies" below. Matt loved it.

Once Liz made a life-size papier-mâché model of a woman standing about five-foot-eight, with a shelf hidden in her belly that housed a tape recorder. Liz had recorded a quiz with questions and answers on it for a school project. Matt adopted "Linda," as he called her, and she became one of the family after her school days were over. The following Hallowe'en Linda stood out on our front porch screaming and dying at kids who came for goodies. Matt had put his tape recorder to use again. But I hadn't used the recorder as a teaching tool until Judy Ball lent us the auditory-discrimination tapes. They are harder to reproduce than drawings.

One of the characteristics of (some) l.d. people is an inability to sift out the important noises from the unimportant noises that surround them. As I write this, there is, of course, the noise of my computer. There is also a power mower on the other side of the building. There is the noise of a fountain in the front garden. There are a few muted voices of people talking in the driveway. A delivery truck just drove up. But I manage (somehow) to concentrate on what I am doing, typing at least eighty mistakes a minute.

An l.d. person has trouble selecting the relative importance of what he hears. He gives equal attention to the commands of his teacher and to the kids whispering behind him, as well as to the street noises outside the schoolroom window, and whatever other distractions are going on in and around his working area. Such a child is called highly distractible, but it's a form of the damage he has suffered and can't be scolded away. Admonitions to concentrate don't help much, and anger or punishment simply adds to his tension.

I read recently about a demonstration inflicted upon a group of parents and educators to show them what it felt like to be unable to discriminate between noises. They were required to sit between two public-address speakers that broadcasted two entirely different messages, each in the same calm voice. It was impossible to listen to both at the same time, and maddening trying to single out one of them to focus on. How does a child choose the one message he is supposed to hear in a room full of noises he can't shut out? That's an auditory example.

You can find a visual example of the kind of frustration l.d. kids experience in an exercise at the Ontario Science Centre in Toronto. It involves the use of a stylus that can only be used with the aid of a mirror. Thus, one is looking at the reflected image of what one is doing and not at the thing itself. The assignment is to outline the shape of a star with the stylus. If you go off the line a buzzer sounds. The commentary concludes, "How would you like to be a dentist?" The real question is, "How would you like to be brain-damaged?"

Anyway, to go back to that problem of auditory discrimination: I was able to reproduce the first tapes myself. I would turn on the tape recorder, put a record on Matt's little record-player, and then read some directions into the tape, instructing Matt to draw something or build a tower with such-and-such colour blocks, and so on. Later, he would play back the tape and try to sift out my directions from the background noise. After that, it got harder. Judy lent me the tapes. Several different sources of noise would be on the tapes, and some of them would have confusing overlaps: two voices each counting out numbers, only one set of which the child is supposed to be listening to.

Using the tape in that way led me to other discoveries. Nothing is as patient as a tape recorder (except, possibly, a computer). I started leaving directions on the tape for Matt to do exercises in my absence. Another thing l.d. kids need a lot of practice with is following directions. One command is all right; two get confusing; three are downright impossible. So I would start slowly, saying, "Take a blue block and put it in front of you. Then take a yellow block and put it on the right side of the blue block. Take a green block and put it on top of the blue and yellow blocks." And so on. That's not only good for directions, it's great for spatial relations. Behind, in front of, on top of, right, left, and so on are very difficult concepts for some of these children. Anything that reinforces and helps with the development of directional and spatial understanding is also a good thing. And, as I say, the tape recorder is much more patient than a human being. It never changes its tone, it never becomes rushed or hurried or exasperated. The child can play the tape over and over again until he gets his instructions right. It really is wonderful. At last I could go out for an evening and not worry that I had let Matthew down by not doing something constructive with him. That was a good feeling.

Judy Ball started Matt on all the standard speech-therapy exercises, concentrating on certain sounds that people with speech problems find very difficult, like *l*, *th*, *ch*, *r*, and *sh*. I made a speech book for Matthew full of three-dimensional illustrations, pop-ups, push-outs, lift-ups, paste-ins, textures, jokes, real-life stories and props. I got carried away, but it was fun to do with Matt and fun for him to learn with. Too many teaching books are so dreary, no fun for the pupil or the teacher. Almost by osmosis, Matthew learned to speak better, too.

From sounds, Judy Ball progressed to grammar. She started teaching Matt his pronouns — *he*, *she*, *it* — and his tenses. He worked very well with her, and learned a lot more in his hour or so every Friday than during the rest of the week put together, or so it seemed to me.

Matt went to most of the plays at Stratford, and whether or not he understood them all, he certainly learned how to behave in a theatre. I would ask him about the story line after, or ask him to tell me about it, as it is suggested one do with all movies and performances an l.d. person sees, to help reinforce the experience and to teach him to express himself clearly. The only problem with that is that I hate to hear a story rehashed!

All these things sound like normal, natural things to do, but in Matt's case I had learned to make each event become something very special—not work, I hope, but an opportunity for learning and for an awareness of learning. It's called enrichment now, and every child can profit by it. There's a book I picked up through The Association for Children with Learning Disabilities called *Listen, My Children, and You Shall Hear*, designed to train a child's memory and communication skills. It is a series of stories told at first, second, and third level, that is, degrees of complexity and length. The stories are supposed to be read aloud to the child (pre-school through grade four) and then the child is asked to tell the story back as well as he can. It's harder than it sounds. Try it yourself.

Well, as I say, therapy becomes a way of life. During the day, or during the year, every event becomes an occasion to celebrate, to mark with special games and projects. You would have thought my middle name was Hallmark! Christmas, as you might expect, was a blowout. I bought out the craft stores in early November and set all the kids to creating their own handcrafted presents for all their long-suffering, tolerant relatives. (Actually, I tried to think of things that were useful to the recipients as well.) We all sat together in the family room day after day just a-cuttin' and a-pastin' and a-snippin'. At Easter time, the same room was awash with Easter egg dye. It was fun for all of us and therapy for Matt.

I would make him a big calendar with a box for each day, to cancel with a big x, and mark off the days until Christmas. This killed several birds, of course: it taught numbers, time, days of the week, and patience. I would print the activity—or draw it—in each box before I crossed it out, and I would count the number of days remaining, naming the days, and ask Matt to count and say them with me.

Lots of mothers with normal children are opportunistic in this way. They repeat in whole sentences what the child has said. They comment on what they are looking at, identifying it with words. They verbalize the child's feelings for him, giving him handles for expression. It's even better, according to child psychologists, if they ask questions, thus eliciting further responses from the child. This is called "verbal tag" and is more effective than verbatim repetitions of what the child has just said.

I listen to young mothers now, on the street and in shopping plazas. The ones who pay this kind of attention to their children, I notice, are rewarded with attentive, rapt, and very well-behaved kids. The ones who keep saying, "Shut up," or "Do you want a smack in the head?" have kids who whine and pull at them and run wild. Don't take my word for it. Go and listen for yourself.

Swings, ladders, balls, sandboxes, all these big-motor playthings take on new meaning when you have a learning-disabled child because all are the tools of therapy. Equipment is important, but more important is the time spent on such therapy. There are body-awareness programs now, including one guerrilla course I saw that kids had to go through every morning. I tried one section of it myself, crawling and wriggling on my stomach under an obstacle less than a foot from the floor. (It's a wonder my rear end cleared it!) Some dance and drama schools have special body training that might be helpful for gross-motor coordination. You'll have to find out what's available in your area, and then find out if your child is welcome or will feel at ease. The programs are often not designed for l.d. kids, and he might have trouble keeping up with the others. That's the trouble with most of the Y gym courses across the country. Even the lowest common denominators, the fat, clumsy kid and the klutz, are still often more adept than your awkward, uncoordinated child.

I know one mother with a son older than Matthew, who thought a trampoline was the answer. It certainly helped her son. He developed, or had developed for him, a whole series of exercises he performed on the trampoline, all involving right-left balance and hand-eye coordination, and near-distant focusing, all designed to improve his reading skills. It worked, or something did, because the boy eventually earned a college degree and is now teaching.

Universities and community colleges, by the way, are more understanding than they used to be. Not all of them accept learning-disabled students, but those that do allow the use of tape recorders both for exams and for lectures, plus extra time to write exams (and sometimes the use of a typewriter). If and when your child is ready for university or community college, ask around and find out which ones make these concessions to the learning disabled. Even bright l.d. students have to work three times as hard as a normal student, and that takes more time, so it's important to have these allowances made.

Well, we didn't have a trampoline but we used to go to a lot of playgrounds, and my other children liked that, too. We became connoisseurs of playgrounds, in fact, liking one for its merry-go-round (the wooden kind you get started by running with it), another for its slide, another for its rustic fort, another for its swings, and so on. I don't go into playgrounds any more, but I notice in passing that some are very imaginative now. And they're free. That's an important consideration when you realize how the cost of all this therapy adds up.

I was buying toys and equipment and books like crazy, trying to learn how to develop and stimulate new areas of that dear, damaged brain of Matthew's. In spite of my *idée fixe* about it, I like to think that all this fussing made me a better mother. It certainly made me a better teacher. I taught Sunday school for years. It became second nature to me to see the way a lesson could become a game, and any event a learning experience. As I said, a way of life.

So maybe therapy is a healing process, after all, not only for the person receiving it but also for the therapist. You have this vital sense of urgency all the time, the feeling that you are doing something positive for your child. Somehow, that feeling helps to ease the constant pressure. It might seem to others that you're merely sitting in the sun watching your child on the swings, or that you could be working when you're kneeling on the floor helping to put stickers in a sticker book. You know better. You're doing therapy, and it's hard to say who for.

CHAPTER FIVE

FAMILY

When the focus of a book is on a child who has a special problem, the emphasis threatens not only the balance of the book but the impression of the family. We were, after all, a normal family, coping with colds, dental appointments, birthday parties, hockey games, music lessons, scraped knees, broken limbs (one – Matthew's arm: he slipped on some ice), and all the usual things that happen to families in the throes of life. What happens to an ordinary family when an extraordinary child is put into its midst is that its members go on living – quite happily. We were all very busy, as families are. Matthew's problems forced us to take extra time for him and that time together benefited us all.

Liz has always had a special relationship with Matt, perhaps because she is the oldest. I never knew until I heard her say it on television, when she was invited to comment on the reactions of a sibling to a special child in the house, how she felt about Matt as "burden" and my husband and me as burden-layers. I guess I was so intent at the time, it never occurred to me to worry about it. It should have. As it turned out, it was okay – in Liz's case, anyway. Certainly, all the children helped with Matthew, and Liz has stated that his life did not curtail her own. She hates games, though.

As Matt grew older, we started playing games to improve his counting and other skills. Every night after dinner, I'd say, "Who wants to play a game?" and gather up volunteers. We became a games-playing family, part of our togetherness. Liz has played too many games in her life.

But she didn't mind getting into the tub with Matthew to help him – until we moved to Stratford when John shared a shower with him. It was fun for Liz and her little brother, and she received one of the first glimpses of the personality Matt was beginning to exhibit.

"Where's the soap?" she said one night, hunting for it. Matt giggled.

"I can't find the soap," said Liz, swishing the water with her hands. Matt giggled again, and handed it to her. He had been sitting on it, deliberately hiding it from her.

You may think that's a tiny, silly incident, but it was very meaningful to us. Liz's slow little brother had played a trick on her! We were all delighted.

One Christmas holiday in Stratford, we took the children and several friends' families on a sleigh ride and back for cider and chili. On the way home, the kids were stacked like cordwood in the back of the station wagon, and the steam on the windows made it hard for the driver to see. One of my kids suddenly shouted out, "Look, look! Look what Matt has done!"

Matt giggled. Everyone looked. Liz, Kate, and John Wylie all ooh'd and ah'd while the other kids in the car wondered what was so special. Matt had written his name in the steam on a car window. It was the first time he had ever written his name other than on a workbook when required. We were all thrilled for him, and he was very proud and pleased with the attention he was getting for it.

John was too young himself to care whether his little brother had a sense of humour or could write his name. All he knew was that Matthew couldn't play with him. Maybe he doesn't consciously remember all those times when he sat on the top bunk wistfully watching me play/work with Matt, but the memory and the unexpressed resentment must still be in his subconscious. And John, being closest to Matthew in age, was not only deprived of a playmate but also suffered embarrassment for his slow brother. Defensive, even belligerent, he would fight tigers to protect Matthew from harm. (The principal of the elementary school told me he had given his teachers orders to look the other way if they saw

John protecting Matthew with his fists.) But John himself could never learn patience with Matthew, and still hasn't. I suppose he feels unconsciously that Matt has cheated him of too much.

It's something to watch for when you have a special child. The child's needs can easily overwhelm the family or dwarf the other children's growth. It must be very hard on a bright, younger child to be constantly made to defer to an older, slower brother, or to be held back because of him.

All my children were changed because Matthew entered our lives. Although Liz never resented Matthew, she does feel that she suffered most because of my unrecognized and repressed anger at the deal I had been handed. Looking back, I know I felt under constant pressure to make each day meaningful and productive for Matt. I was also under pressure to produce for myself. All my life I had wanted to write. I had blithely promised myself that when my last child entered school I would start trying to write "full-time." Well, not full-time exactly, but during school hours, in what time could be spared from my household cares and social obligations.

But my last child's schooling was going to be problematical for a long, long time. I could see that. And his teachers weren't going to be able to teach him enough. Someone would have to fill in the incredible gaps in his learning process. That someone was me. What other choice was there?

Self-imposed or not, the pressure raised my stress level and lowered my tolerance. That's when I began incubating my ulcer, first diagnosed in 1967 as an "acid stomach." Oh, my, yes—acid! But the funny pain I used to think was a heavy chest began before Matt was two years old. I just didn't know what that was. Anyway, the acid eroded not only my stomach but my relationship with my oldest daughter.

I have heard of other relationships destroyed by the presence of a special child in the family. Often marriages falter and fail. Frequently, the anger of the damaged one breaks out when he is older and he lashes out at his siblings. I know of one l.d. young man who beats up his sister regularly. Others simply drift away, glad to be rid of the pressures and demands of the family. Every family has a scapegoat. In a family with a special child, the scapegoat is not automatically that child. It depends on the shifts and variations within each structure. Liz, as I said, feels she was the scapegoat, suffering the brunt of my frustration and pain. John, on the other hand, got the full impact of my neglect.

John was a resourceful, bright boy, though, and I found things for him to learn and grow with. He was isolated by his position in the family, with two older sisters who teamed up to tease him, and without a normal younger brother to rally to his defence, with a busy father and a harassed mother. But he has become a wonderful human being. Does it help to know that while a problem child will certainly present difficulties and pain, he will also provide opportunities for growth and heightened sensitivity that might never have developed?

Number-two daughter, Kate, seemed to be the least affected by Matthew. She found friends outside the family and remains to this day warm and loving, with an easy, relaxed attitude and an astonishing number of friends. She was the one who always befriended strays, the one for whom we installed a children's telephone for her counselling hours, who helped out with the swimming classes I set up for l.d. kids in Stratford, who taught riding to mentally handicapped kids when she was at university (and she didn't even know how to ride herself), and who worked with a crisis centre, too, during the years she studied for her honours psychology degree. She's as quick and impatient as I am, though, and her tension is hidden and erupts in similar outlets. Is it genetic, or was it bred by the pressures imposed by a household centred around the needs of a handicapped child?

So characters and lifestyles change when you have a handicapped child. The focus of the family shifts, necessarily. You have to be aware of the stress on the other members as well as on yourself. In a way, mother and child are at the centre of the storm, closely involved with each other. What happens to the others? What about the husband?

I know a father who had a son with far fewer difficulties than Matthew had, but who found it difficult to recognize any problems at all. Once he read a magazine article about dyslexia and wondered whether his son's difficulties with reading might stem from that, but he didn't know what to do about it, except leave it to very competent teachers in the private school he enrolled his son in. These teachers, and smaller classes and extra time and attention, certainly did help to compensate for the boy's deficiencies. But no matter what you do, whether you hide from it or try to ignore it, the problem raises its unavoidable head by grade ten—it's like a magic wall that can't be climbed. That's the level beyond which these kids cannot progress, not without highly skilled assistance. That's the level at which the delinquency and the drop-outs begin, it seems. This man's son left school at grade ten.

I know another man whose third son was absolutely incapable of following in the footsteps of his high-achieving siblings, both of them in medical school while he was struggling with grade ten for the third or fourth time. The father was a professional man himself and no son of his was going to be a blue-collar worker. He pulled his son out of school and left him with nothing. He was to be a go-fer for the rest of his life, with no training, no contacts, no friends, nothing.

I know of other men who left their marriages, and that's worse, because the entire family is affected. It's true that the stresses and strains placed on a marriage by the presence of a handicapped child are enormous and heartbreaking. As with every other crisis in life, they have to be dealt with openly and honestly, with compassion and love. More love, not less.

But I don't want to be too hard on fathers. Fathers, when disappointed, may not do much for a damaged child. Mothers, when they are too frightened by the odds, abandon the child altogether. The severely retarded children in institutions are usually there because of the decision of the mothers not to keep them. I guess each woman must know her own strength and how far it will spread, especially when there are other children or a demanding husband to take care of.

It's hard to be relaxed with a problem child. If we could just learn to love them more and worry less, we'd all be better off. But we need a little help with that. A little more information would help; so would a network of friends, of para-professionals, of counsellors and guides. Certainly, damaged children need all the help they can get, but so, often, do their parents.

I always thought Bill Wylie was perfect, though he wasn't, of course. He really did leave too much of the burden of Matthew to me. There were skills he could have helped Matt with—ball-throwing and -catching, obstacle courses, and balance-board walking — while I was cooking dinner, for example. He seldom did that. But did I want him to? When he came home I was glad that he wanted to talk to me, to tell me about his day. To me, that was as important as any therapy he could have been doing with Matthew.

Then, too, he was totally involved in the theatre work he was doing by that time. He was finding it very satisfying and exciting, and he was discovering how good he was at it. He had little attention or energy to spare for ball-throwing. He gave me a great deal of emotional support and financial help. He never protested at the amount of money I spent on educational toys and equipment.

Bill didn't have the false pride that many men have that makes them unable to acknowledge the fact that they have a handicapped child. It seems to be especially hard for men to face if the child is a son, as it usually is, and even harder if it's the only boy. They feel cheated of their immortality with a damaged, possibly end-of-the-line boy. Bill was not only a humble man but a realistic one — and he had another son. So he was able to accept Matthew's disability, maybe too readily. He made no special provision for Matt's special needs, nor was he willing to finance an exploration into special education. Perhaps to say unwilling is unfair. We didn't have much money and we had three other children.

But he was always willing to play games with the group after dinner and he performed all kinds of loving, unsung services for all of us, easing the pressure where it most needed to be eased. He could solve a problem, if I could define and present it to him. For example, when Matthew was only four months old and still taking an enormous amount of time to nurse and care for, I wanted to have a birthday party for Liz, but couldn't see how to squeeze it in between feedings.

"Easy," said Bill, "we'll take the kids on a train ride. Then you just have to feed them and send them home."

None of the seven-year-olds, as it turned out, had ever had a train ride. Bill took them to Transcona, the first stop outside Winnipeg on the Trans-Canada line, a ride of some twenty minutes. He took a babysitter with him in case any of his charges (all female) needed to go to the bathroom on the train, and he arranged for a friend with a camper to meet the train in Transcona and drive our guests back to our place — for breakfast, as it turned out. Because the train left Winnipeg at 8:20 in the morning! It was the strangest invitation, and party, and one that few of Liz's friends' mothers have ever forgotten. The children arrived at eight o'clock and were whisked off to the train station, back at nine for a barbecued breakfast, home and ready for the day by ten-thirty. It was the ideal party for a nursing mother to have, and it was all my husband's idea. That's the kind of imaginative help I could always count on him to provide.

If I seem to be focusing outward with myself as the centre point, that's partly because this book is written from my point of view. It is also because mothers seem to get more involved than fathers with their handicapped children. In the past, it has been because the stay-at-home housewife had that kind of time, and the responsibility seemed to be hers. Father's work, as well as his pride, often prevented him from doing very much for his child on a regular basis. Perhaps this is no longer true, as fathers are learning to take on a more nurturing role in the family.

There is a danger in having a mother like me. Judy Ball, Matt's speech therapist, pointed out to me the advantages and disadvantages to a child of having me for a mother and a background like Matt's. While he profited from such an enriched environment, Matthew was also constantly aware of how far he fell short of my/our standards and what little chance he had of reaching that level of performance. On the other hand, he has developed a strong sense of self and wonderful poise, though I am aware that sometimes he looks to me too much for affirmation. My fault for being too strong. He's learning to deal with that, too, with humour.

Once, before Matt was in school full-time, so that must have been our first spring in Stratford, when he was seven years old and fairly tall for his age so that people wondered what he was doing out of school during school hours, I took him with me to the Stratford Music Festival to hear the other kids sing. I was wondering as we got out of the car who would say, "What's a big boy like you doing here?" and feeling a bit sorry for myself. At the same time, I was ashamed of my disloyalty to Matt, and to make up for it, I said out loud to him, "I really like you, Matt." And he nodded happily and said, "Yeah, everyone does."

You see, he never stopped teaching me. He is his own unique self, with a strong sense of self, and he likes himself, and other people like him, too. He has problems, heaven knows. We all have problems. But Matthew knows who he is, and he's glad to be here. I'm glad he is, too.

There are other mothers, smarter than I am, with a wisdom of the heart, who don't need to learn this because they already know it. They simply accept each child for what he or she is. I had to learn that.

What happens outside the family has to be handled with humour and understanding, too. Well-meaning relatives have to be guided. Often they have to be persuaded not to treat a special child like a child forever. I finally spoke to one aunt who persisted in calling Matthew "Mattie" for years after it ceased to be appropriate. And Matthew finally spoke to another aunt, shocking her, I'm afraid, when he said, "Why do you talk to me like I was four years old?" (He was seventeen at the time.) Grandparents and relatives tend to want to wrap a handicapped child in cotton batting. You can't do that. No one else does. Sooner or later, they have to face the world, and it's a harsh one.

The other thing that relatives tend to do is to hide their heads in the sand and refuse to believe that anything is wrong with the child. My mother did that for years with Matthew. After every visit to the doctor I would report to her. Before I could finish she would interrupt, saying, "But he's all right, isn't he? He's all right." No, he wasn't all right. If he had been all right, he wouldn't have been going to the developmental diagnostician in the first place.

It's fear, it's concern, it's an unwillingness to face the fact that there's anything wrong with your family. Both you and your relatives have to understand quite clearly that there is, indeed, something wrong. Grandparents mean well, but you may have to spell things out for them, as well as you can, and help them understand that there really is a problem and it's not going to go away. You can't ignore it. You — and your child, with your help — will have to learn to live with it. So he has problems. It's not the end of the world. Nothing is, except the end of the world.

There's an even more frightening attitude that occurs sometimes within the families of severely handicapped children. That is a kind of unspoken assumption that the child has died. Some parents actually mourn the loss of the child they might have had — that is, of the normal child they wanted. They surround the child with "flowers" — excessive praise — and with epitaphs — "if Jimmy had been normal, he might have...." As I have said, if-onlys are impossible to live with. It is a temptation, but avoid hanging wreaths of if-onlys around your child's neck. Some parents even go so far as to whitewash the tomb; they try to be nice all the time. They paint too-bright pictures, they hide their grief and disappointment, and, yes, rage.

It is human to be angry. It is human to hate your child. Not all the time, mind you, but it is human. (I will tell you in another chapter when I hated Matt most.) Even normal children are sometimes hated by their parents. Most of us manage to control our negative feelings and stop short of child abuse. But I can understand the desperation and weariness that could lead a less-fortunate person than I was to an excess of physical rage. All I have to do is remember what it was like to have four very young children and to have been up all night with one of them. Dying for lack of sleep, I had a very short fuse the next day. I did not strike a child, but I sure screamed and ranted a lot. It doesn't make me very proud to admit that, but truth must out.

I think maybe it's not a bad thing if you go ahead and tell your child that he pisses you off. It may make you both feel better in the long run, especially if you give him space and permission to be pissed off with you, too. I'm sure he has some complaints as well.

But don't dwell on them. If things get too tough for both of you, take a holiday from each other. In Toronto there are "relief homes" run by the Metropolitan Toronto Association for the Mentally Retarded expressly for that purpose, to give parents of severely retarded children a break from the constant care and frustration and worry. Check the facilities in your city and find out if there is such a service available. If there isn't, then make arrangements with a trusted relative or friend to take your child — even for an hour of two, but preferably longer — so that you can get a break.

The older the child, the more difficult it is to make such arrangements. I had many different solutions over the years. One effective one, when Matt was older, was to invite a university student, usually a close friend of one of my other children, to come and live in. These friends were near enough to Matthew in age that he didn't feel insulted by being "babysat," and the students didn't feel too tied down because Matt could do a lot for himself. Some kids can't, of course.

When the boys were much younger, after the girls had gone away to school, I solved the problem one winter by trading room and board for the presence of a student. I required no housework or services other than her presence during my absence when she would have to provide herself and the boys with meals (already cooked, in my freezer). By that time I was starting to write professionally and had to be away a lot. That worked very well, and the fact that the young woman was a public health nurse (saving for a trip to Europe) gave me added peace of mind.

There is always a solution to a problem if you make up your mind that there is, and don't give up. The point is that it is probably more important that you take a break once in a while from a special child than from a so-called normal child.

But this is assuming constant tension, which no one can live with for very long. You simply have to stop and smell the flowers as you go by. Oddly enough, with a special child, there are lots of flowers and lots of opportunity to enjoy them. (Therapy, remember?) Life is irrelevant, thank goodness, and bestows gifts and moments of relief and laughter when you least expect it. I'm sure you can think of many such moments in your life, but I'll tell you a few of my favourites.

I used to keep a big memo board attached to the side of my fridge for all of us to write reminders on—groceries, supplies, things we needed. After Matt could write, he used the board, too, and one day I found this message on it: SWON BOTS. I thought they sounded like the seven-league boots you'd find in a fairy tale. What Matt needed were new snow boots.

Another time he wrote down the names of his sisters and brother as ZIT, KAE, and FOT. Liz, Kate, and John have used those names in jest ever since. They have become part of the folklore of our family jokes.

It took us all a long time to teach Matthew how to ride a bicycle. My husband and all the kids took turns running behind him with one hand on the saddle to keep him balanced until he learned. (One thing you learn with a special child: it may seem like forever, but they do eventually learn.) Fortunately, we lived on a court—a circular street—so that no runner or cyclist ever got too far from the house. All the neighbours learned to slow down as they entered the court so as not to hit the learner. It was a celebration for the whole street when Matt finally balanced by himself. When the last hand let go of his saddle, neighbours came out to watch him go by as if he were a parade.

Shoelaces were even more dramatic, though. Matt had tried for years to learn to tie shoelaces and simply couldn't master that intricate art. As I mentioned earlier, I tried to ease the social pressure of the problem by buying him loafers, but he had to return to a shoe with better support. Finally — he was about nine years old — the teacher in his special education class told him not to return after the Christmas holidays if he hadn't mastered shoelace-tying by the time they were over. Well, he tried, but the night before he was supposed to return to school, he still couldn't get his poor, unresponsive, clumsy fingers to cooperate. We all sat around him, encouraging him, each showing him something that might finally help him, but nothing worked. The girls and I were in tears; John got glasses of water for all of us to comfort us because it was the only thing he could think of doing to help. Bill tried to cheer us all up. There was no help for it. Matt would have to go to school the next day still unable to tie his shoelaces.

The next night, however, he finally did it, and we were all so happy for him. I guess it's moments like that that cement a family. It also proves something else: as much as you want to do everything you can for your child, in the long run he has to be able to do for himself. No one but Matt could tie his shoelaces. Ultimately, they were his problem.

Liz commented once, watching Matthew read, that it looked as if he were slowly going through a Rolodex file in his head. She said that if she had to go through what he had to go through, she'd be out of her skull. Yes, well, we'll get to that.

You keep forgetting though. Once you have accepted a handicap and learned to live with it, structured your life around it, and kept moving with it, you forget it. No member of a close, loving family can live in isolation from it. Matt was a vital, integral part of our group. We didn't constantly make allowances for him. Once the basic ground rules were established, we all lived with them. When we played games, we played to win, and Matt developed a keen sense of the jugular. He's a whiz at Concentration; he always beats me at Monopoly (everyone does), and his understanding of poker is lethal. Of course, we didn't try to play Scrabble or Probe with him, but there were many games where he could hold his own, no quarter given or expected.

That's what family life is about, I think. Certainly you make allowances for the weakest link in the chain, but you don't stop living, you don't stop loving. The Wylie family was making steady progress.

CHAPTER SIX

SCHOOLING

For most parents of children with learning disabilities, this book begins here. Throughout the pre-school period doubts are often brushed aside and hopes pinned on the magic therapy of school. "Just wait until he gets to school. He'll be all right then."

If you have older children, your fears have had comparisons to feed on because the others didn't behave like this when they were your special child's age. If the special child is a first child, then any shortcomings or problems you have already noticed become a reason to blame yourself. Other people are quite ready to blame you, too. You've probably noticed that already.

"You're spoiling him," one or another relative will say. "You should be firmer with him. What he needs is discipline." Or attention. Or neglect. Or love. Or time. School will change all that, you hope. The teachers will know what to do.

Don't be too sure.

In the first place, your child may not be ready for school. If, however, his problems have never been diagnosed, it's likely that neither you nor the school will know that. So you'll give him a pencil and a kiss, cross your fingers, and send him off. It's going to be a shock for everyone concerned. Brace yourself.

Depending on the severity of your child's problems and the degree to which he is able to mask them, he will start running head-on into the system sooner or later. Suddenly, nothing is simple. By this time, you may have learned to live with what you called his stubborn streak, or his short attention span, or his spasms of wild behaviour. You know he needs extra time, space, and fewer distractions to help him function well. Lots of parents know this about their children without knowing they have a learning disability. But this kind of lenience is often what a teacher can least afford to grant. She has a system. She has thirty other kids to push through kindergarten. Or grade one. Or grade two. With borderline problem kids, a lot of teachers will simply try to push them through the system and ignore the basic problems, hoping that at some time in the future the kid will grow out of them, or that someone else will find a way to cope with them.

In the meantime, if he wasn't before, the child becomes a behaviour problem. Frustrated, baffled, failing, or failing to understand, he gets criticized, ignored, scolded, and taunted. Soon he quits trying, refuses to make an effort, or to respond at all. He is accused of faking it, of being stubborn, lazy, stupid, or deliberately annoying. He can't help it, but no one seems to realize that.

This is the classic case of the undiscovered brain-damaged kid, who hits school like a battering-ram — with his head. There are one million kids like him in Canada, according to the CELDIC (Commission on Emotional and Learning Disorders in Children) report, *One Million Children*, published in 1970. In this national study of children with emotional and learning disorders, the following children were considered:

- children who are neurotic or psychotic
- children with an overall learning deficit — the retarded
- children with specific learning difficulties or deficits
- children with sensory or physical handicap likely to lead to a secondary emotional or learning problem
- children who are judged to be delinquent
- children whose family or community experience leads to cultural or emotional deprivation

It was estimated then that 12 per cent of the population up to nineteen years of age — that is, a million children and youths in Canada — required attention, treatment, and care because of emotional and learning disorders. The figure is probably higher now, if only because the problems have names and the children can be identified more readily.

But how swiftly or accurately the children's problems are identified varies greatly, not only from province to province, but from city to city and town to town. Psychometrists, that is, people who measure the mental state and processes of a student, are still rare and in demand. A lot of teachers don't even ask for testing, so the students remain undiagnosed, though not unnoticed.

Thus, obtaining testing and a diagnosis is often the first hurdle parents must overcome in order to put a name to their child's problems. Even if they've beaten a path to the school and have the best points for attendance at all the home-and-school meetings, the principal and the teacher are likely to groan inwardly at the sight of them. The school doesn't know what's going to become of the kid, either. Teachers are usually overworked, with too many students and too little time for them. It is easier to neglect the brights and the slows. It saves time that way, and it saves more time if you don't know what their problem is. Besides, who has the equipment necessary to deal with them, anyway? School boards across the country are notoriously reluctant to spend money on special education. If you tested everyone who had a complaint, you'd just be opening up another can of wriggly problems.

There are private organizations now that will do some testing — for a fee. The best way to find the good ones is to consult your nearest Association for Children with Learning Disabilities. At least, everything is closer and a little less expensive than it used to be. I know one woman who fought her son's battles from kindergarten to grade eight and right through high school until she found a diagnostician in Montreal (she lived in Toronto) who finally put a name to the boy's problem and set up a therapy program for him. Long before double-income families were common, this woman went to work to supplement her husband's income so that they could pay for all the extra help their son required.

Special lessons, special therapy, tutorial help, and finally special schools, all take money. There is some government aid (usually provincial) available. But even if you can get it, it is available only after the fact. You find the school, you pay for it, then you apply for assistance. There's a cut-off age, however, at which point the child is no longer legally a child and therefore no longer qualifies for such aid. Never mind if he's reading at the grade-three level. He's twenty-one; he should get a job. How?

Don't be too discouraged if you can't afford special schooling. Most of the best schools are in the United States, anyway, and there aren't many of them.

As for the special-education classes within the school system, they are frequently geographically removed from where the child lives. One class may comprise pupils from several different schools in the region. The classroom is frequently chosen only for the simple fact that it happens to be empty. Convenience of access has nothing to do with it. Once the class exists, it can become a kind of dumping ground: children with a wide range of disabilities may be placed in it because it's there, and so are they. In Matt's first special-ed class, for example, there were learning-disabled kids, whose disabilities ranged from mild to severe, hyperactive kids, a couple of emotionally disturbed kids, and one severe epileptic. But I'm getting ahead of myself.

Matthew was not ready for school even with the six months' lead he had by being a February baby. He had gone to St. George's Nursery School two mornings a week when he was three, three mornings a week when he was four, but when he was five and a half and theoretically ready to begin kindergarten, his developmental diagnostician said he wasn't ready and prescribed the high-quality daily pre-school class that all my friends' children had gone to at St. Andrews (United) Church. We ended up changing churches (not denominations) in order to get Matt in, and he spent a good, productive year there.

After that the doctor wanted to see if the system he had helped to set up was working. So he asked me not to volunteer any extra information about Matthew when I registered him for kindergarten. If the system was working, the teacher would notice the lag in Matt's development, and his difficulties, and put a call through for an assessment and help for Matt. The call did not go through.

I had a play produced that year, the fall of 1967. As I noticed a change in Matthew's behaviour, I blamed myself, thinking that it was my busyness and absences that were the cause of it. Then I realized that as far as Matt was concerned, my hours were such that he was not even much aware of my absence. He was still getting my attention every afternoon as always, doing our games and exercises. But he was irritable and becoming more and more hesitant and unsure of himself and even reluctant to go to school—which he had never been before.

One day late that fall I found out why. The kindergarten teacher invited the parents (read mothers) to see the kids and her in action. I was shocked. It seemed to me that she practised overt favouritism and discrimination. Children who couldn't handle their buttons or shoelaces had to wait for help that was a long time coming and was neither graceful nor generous when it came. In the teacher's defense, I will say that she had too many pupils in her room, and a very short time to go to retirement. She was probably much more tired than the children by the end of the morning or afternoon.

Some of her ideas worked well in theory, if one was working with normally achieving children. For example, to leave, the children had to say a word beginning with a letter of the alphabet (there were more than twenty-six children in the class; when they reached Z they began again). The bright ones with their As, Bs, and Cs were out the door like a shot. Matt was lucky to get out with a W or an X. And I had wondered why he was so slow coming home from school.

This is where his tension began and grew. My little fella, who had had nothing but encouragement and patience and understanding, was getting a taste not only of failure—he knew what that was like, but in a supportive atmosphere—but of failure accompanied by ridicule from his swifter classmates, and by imposed competition and unstated but obvious and odious comparisons.

I was furious, and glad we were moving away from the problem. My husband was a theatrical yo-yo during the fall of 1967. He was appointed general manager of the Stratford Festival Theatre, with an overlapping responsibility at the Manitoba Theatre Centre until a successor was found. We had thought to stay on for the entire school year in Winnipeg and move in June of 1968. But one night I looked at all the unhappy faces at the dinner table, no doubt reflecting mine, and decided we would move between Christmas and New Year's. Actually, we moved to Stratford on January 1, 1968.

Matthew and the others were duly registered at their respective schools, and we began to adjust to a new community. I did in

Stratford as the doctor had recommended I do in Winnipeg, and gave no extra information about Matt. I waited to see what the system could do.

I was dazzled. Two days after Matt started at his new school, a public health nurse called, on recommendation of his kindergarten teacher, to find out his background and see how they might help him. Actually, there wasn't much help, I mean, sophisticated help, but the kindergarten teacher was outstanding. Matt finished his first year of kindergarten much more happily than he began.

Throw away the calendar. Starting one-and-a-half years late to kindergarten, Matt went the full day — to kindergarten in the morning and grade one in the afternoon — for the next year. He got two of everything; all the parties were duplicated. The next year he was allowed to go all day to grade one, and a remedial teacher came for two forty-five-minute sessions a week and taught him to read. He was ahead of his slow group in grade one because of the extra time and attention he received.

The next year, at age nine and a half, he was put into a special-education class out of his district. A dear and helpful friend of mine who lived close to that school had him for lunch every day. So began a long and varied school career, one that is still continuing, still being agonized over, evaluated, assessed, and questioned. As I say, throw away the calendar.

I had realized long since, however, that though you might throw away the chronological calendar as far as a special child's progress is concerned, the child, nevertheless, keeps making progress. This is true for Down's-syndrome children, too. Once thought ineducable, they are astonishing educators and parents with the amount they can learn and the confidence they can achieve.

Because Matthew's problems were multiple and apparent and because we knew of them from such an early age, there was no question but that he needed special help all his life. There is, however, a controversy about the kind of special help a special child should receive. Some educators and parents feel very strongly that the child should never be lifted out of his peer group or segregated in any way. They think that "mainstreaming" — that is, keeping the child in the mainstream of the school program — is too valuable to the child to be ignored.

Some children, indeed, feel singled out by special treatment and suffer accordingly. Heaven knows they get teased and taunted enough for their difficulties without being dumped in a wastebasket class of slow learners and problem children. (It depends on the size of the class whether a number of different problems are lumped, or whether kids with matching problems can work together.)

It depends on school boards' decisions, too. Some boards feel that special ed is a frill and should be cut. In that case, mainstreaming is all there is. But mainstreaming without extra funds for equipment or teachers' aides is terribly hard on teachers, as any teacher will tell you.

I keep seeing the disadvantages in special-ed classes as well as in mainstreaming, and I keep changing my mind as to which treatment is more effective for the special child. I think it depends a lot on how much money is available. Ideally, mainstreaming would be best, keeping the child in his home region, abreast as much as possible with his peers, participating in the normal life of the community. But keeping abreast and participating take money and time, and mainstreaming is not always endowed with these two items.

What can a helpless parent do? Join an organization, be active politically—for this is a political issue, ultimately. Ask questions. Nag, even. And then maybe shop around. You may not be able to afford a private school or tutoring, but you might be able to find something better in the public school system than what your child is being given. What I discovered in Matt's kindergarten class is not unique, I'm sure. If such discrimination is going on in the class your child is in, complain, or pull him out. Or if you can't do either of these, then at least be aware of it and find ways to compensate at home for the lacks and assaults at school—not an easy thing to do. Listen, no one ever said any of this was easy.

Both mainstreaming and special-ed classes can work if there is some thought (and money) behind it. A special child needs special equipment. Often it can be very simple and not too expensive, but it can make all the difference to his attention span and to his learning ability. Parents can supply a lot, and do try to make up the gap, but the schools everywhere (read school boards) should realize that the dollars spent on educating a special child will save many more dollars spent on that frustrated youth and young adult as he hits the juvenile-delinquent lists, the welfare lists, the mental-hospital lists, and the hopeless lists. What may seem like a simple case of frustration or a problem he'll "grow out of" in childhood may send a kid into a vicious and ever-widening circle of failure and despair that ruins his life.

I have seen hints in magazine and newspaper stories that the incidence of l.d. kids among juvenile delinquents is very high. Then I have heard arguments stating that the reason for the higher number of convictions is that the l.d. kids can't tell a convincing or logical story about their activities and thus fail to get off as frequently as does a "normal" (I hate that word!) kid.

Similarly, I have heard and read that the incidence of mental breakdown among l.d. youth is much higher than among normal kids. But when I consulted some experts about this, they made light of these rather frightening reports, saying that there are no statistics to support this idea, and that mental illness can happen to any young (or old) person under stress. So, what about the stress? A lot of children with a simple learning disability — if such a thing is ever simple — will find their initial problem compounded by an emotional one if they run head-on into an unsympathetic teacher or school system, or if they have unreasonable and demanding parents. But who knows? Personally, I think that all the returns aren't in. I am told that the number of mentally handicapped people among the mentally ill is increasing all the time.

On the other hand, the same heat that melts wax tempers steel. Parents of l.d. kids will tell you proudly of all the famous people who had a learning disability when they were children, starting with Einstein. He certainly did all right.

Few people can comfort themselves with thoughts of Einstein, however, when their child is being pushed into a special-ed class. There are two things wrong with special-ed classes. One is the segregation. The kid already knows he's got trouble without being singled out like this. He's already suffered the taunts in the playground and the not-so-subtle discrimination in the classroom. Why remove him from his peer group and neighbours? The trouble with special schools is that a special child never has a chance to develop close friends, or any number of them.

His understanding isn't impaired. Some l.d. kids are quite well coordinated and able to participate in most sports and playground activities and hold their own (Matt wasn't). But if they're lifted out of the mainstream, they lose the easy acceptance of the playmates they've been separated from.

The other problem with special-ed classes is just the opposite of that in the mainstream class. Where the teacher in the latter tends to push the kid through because she hasn't the time, equipment, or patience to deal with his problems, the teacher in a special-ed class lets the kid go. No pressure at all. She doesn't have to hand in a roster at the end of the year with the names of the students ready for the next grade. Special-ed classes are ungraded; no one has to meet the June deadline and promotion. So there's not enough incentive for the teacher – or the kid. What happens, I fear, is that the child gets lazy. It's a real temptation. After all, the work is four times harder to cope with than it is for a "normal" child. It's much more pleasant to avoid it, if one can. Avoid or evade. Learning-disabled kids can become very adept at evasion. And no one is pushing them. They get lots of praise, frequently indiscriminate praise, for very little effort. Why not just coast?

Special ed is not the saviour one might think, although at the time that Matthew entered his first full-time special-ed class, I was very grateful. I think it was the thought that at last there was someone who was going to help me with him, someone out there who cared.

So Matthew started to slip through the system, slipping ever further behind, widening the gap every year between his own achievement and the level he might have, could have, should have reached. Who knows? Who knew what was right? Parents are easily cowed by experts. They tend to accept what is being done for their child – until they become uncomfortably aware that perhaps things could be better.

I guess it was when Matt's excellent teacher left his special-ed class to be replaced by a young woman, barely out of teacher's college, with a six-week special-ed summer course to her credit, that I realized that the so-called "experts" dealing with my son didn't know as much as I did by this time. I guess that's when I began to form a Stratford chapter of the Association for Children with Learning Disabilities.

It wasn't easy. There is a very thin layer of executive people in Stratford who sit on all the boards and who are far too busy because there are so few of them. It happened that I was the only one from the white-collar level of education and security who had a problem child. No, there was one other, but her son was much older than Matthew. She had already fought most of her battles. Still, she was a wonderful help. All the other parents of problem kids were blue-collar workers, afraid of challenging the system. I formed an ACLD, all right, but it was an organization that had more strength on paper, in the letters I wrote and the contacts I made, than it did in the people working for it. Still, we managed to set up an after-school recreation program for the kids through the local Y, with swimming classes for them. And we actually hosted a weekend provincial meeting of recreation workers in special ed, with over eighty people attending. Amazing!

This is always what it takes, a concerned parent or parents challenging the system, trying to improve conditions and opportunities for their children. But the costs are sometimes high. What it did to my ulcer was also amazing. I ended up that winter in hospital with my first blood transfusions for bleeding ulcers. I was told to slow down, to cool it. One of the first things I cooled was my ACLD work. The chapter, however, still exists in Stratford; I looked it up in the ACLD directory. I think that proves that no one is indispensable, and my erstwhile ulcer and I are grateful for that.

The organization does good work, not the least in the form of the encouragement it provides, and the realization that one is not alone in dealing with one's problems. The ACLD is a useful guide and source of information, too. For example, you can get a directory of schools for l.d. children from the Ontario ACLD. Write the Association for Children with Learning Disabilities, 1901 Yonge Street, Suite 504, Toronto, Ontario M4S 2Z3.

In the meantime, Matthew went on to another school. King Lear (really) School was a senior public school far away from where we lived. There was such a complicated bus route that he required a taxi service to and from school. (He had taken a school bus to the other special-ed school.) I find such transportation service ironic — that much money spent on a car and driver when school boards get so chintzy about spending money in the classrooms.

By this time, Matt's father had died and his mother was trying to make a living. There was no longer time for the hours of therapy and homework. About the only thing we still did was play games after dinner with the family. And I still read aloud to him, because his understanding was far beyond his own reading skill.

I moved to Toronto in the summer of 1975. I had to find a new school for Matt. By this time I knew the system and knew you had to ask. I took the appropriate papers and went and saw the officials, then the school, and then I came home and taught Matt how to get there by subway. It was a whole new world for him. It was also a very good school. In his two years there, Matt had two excellent teachers. It was still special ed, though, and progress was slow.

Also, let's face it, the extent of his disabilities, and the range of them, really did impede his progress. His first-year teacher told me she had never had a slower (read dumber, read more developmentally handicapped) student in her years in special ed.

But he learned the subway system very quickly, and he had a prodigious memory for things I tended to forget. He took speech therapy every other week at Wellesley Hospital (and learned how to get there, and from there to school in one lesson) and he was the one who always remembered when his next session was. I signed him up for every after-school program there was, because I was working so hard I was frequently not home by the time he was through each day. So he stayed on to take cooking, macramé, floor hockey, acting, and so on. An enriched course, you might say.

Matt "graduated" from grade eight at Jesse Ketchum School. Not from grade eight, really, but from the school, and he was given a diploma at the graduation exercises entitling him to go on to somewhere. By this time he was a recognized school character, and he had suffered for it (we'll get to that). So everyone knew who he was when he went up on the stage to receive his piece of paper. The kids cheered, and Matt—dear, feisty kid that he is—stopped in the middle of the stage, turned to face his audience and pulled "a Fonz"—Heeey! It was a moment of triumph.

Short-lived, I'm afraid. Because I had no idea where he was going to go to school that fall. The closest high school to us, a vocational school within easy walking distance, had no special-ed program. Neither did the tough vocational school on the other side of the ravine. The Toronto School Board had apparently cancelled its special-ed programs in the high schools that year. It was recommended that Matt go to the tough vocational school, but what could he take? He wasn't reading anywhere near the grade-nine level, nor did he have any fine-motor skills that could enable him to take mechanics or carpentry. Worse than that, the school, I was told, was a very tough inner-city school. Matt would get eaten alive. He had already suffered a lot of playground persecution, and I couldn't consciously send him off to a slaughterhouse.

Another complication was that John was going off to university that fall. I had no backup, no one to stay with Matt when I was away, as I was more and more frequently with my work. (My first book, *Beginnings*, was due to be published that fall and I was going on a publicity tour across Canada.) I certainly couldn't afford to send him to a private school, even if I could find one (they're rare).

The solution was presented to me out of an act of kindness by Matt's summer-camp director. He had begun a year-round operation for disturbed l.d. kids, a residence school in southern Ontario. He bent some rules and took Matthew into that school. Matthew was not disturbed and he was not delinquent, as most of the students were. But he needed a place to learn. I trusted the director; he had done a lot for Matt at summer camp. And I had no other choice.

So Matt went off to boarding school the same fall that John went off to university. In one sudden sweep, my last two kids left home. My girls were long gone; my husband was dead. I was alone. I don't do things by halves. I bring it up not because I want you to feel sorry for me, but because I do know what it feels like when that last child, the one you've spent so much time with, leaves. Talk about your empty-nest syndrome! Weekends that Matt didn't make it home, I wrote down a schedule for myself so that I wouldn't sit in a welter of self-pity and loneliness. I checked the movie times and planned at exactly what time I would go to a show. No longer having a child to program, I had a tougher problem. I had to program myself.

Parents who send their special child off to school will feel this way, at whatever age it happens. Think of parents of deaf or blind children who must part with them so much sooner. I remember Liz went to Sunday school with a little blind girl who had to leave home in Winnipeg for a special school in Ontario when she was only six years old. It must have been with a terrible pang that the parents saw that child off. It's an emotional amputation.

The same thing happens to me when I send a child off to camp or to Europe, or anywhere far away or exotic. I guess this kind of separation teaches you that you must love with open hands, always ready to let go.

The school was harsh, as it turned out. My dear camp director imposed a tough behaviour-modification program on his tough l.d. kids. Maybe it worked for them but it was very hard on Matthew. There were point systems for everything, and the students had to earn the right to go home for the weekend. Anything could queer it, not only rebellious behaviour or rule-breaking, but bad schoolwork or apparent failure to pay attention. Often Matthew would go all week doing quite well and then blow it on the Friday and have his weekend cancelled. It was a punishment for me, too, because I was lonely and looked forward to having him home with me. Still, he was looked after and that was important to me because I was away a lot that first fall. And he was making progress in his schoolwork. And the school had an excellent athletic program, something I hadn't been able to provide Matt with, except for our swimming.

So I shut my eyes to other things that bothered me. I had no choice, as I say, but I should have. I should have known. Sometimes, when you need something too much, you blind yourself to the cost and the consequences. I will touch on them now, to try to make other parents aware of some of the questions they should ask, some of the things they should check out, before they send a child off to a residence school.

Behaviour modification is all very well in its way, I suppose, but it must be tailored to the child. Two characteristics of Matthew's did not suit the program he faced. First, he is a very gentle person (usually, and I will go into his and other children's need to express their anger elsewhere) and he does not respond well to harsh treatment. Few children do, actually. Neither do I. Tell me I'm doing a good job and I'll redouble my efforts. Tell me I'm going to fail or that I'm doing miserably, and I cringe and lose my nerve to try again.

Second, like most l.d. kids, Matt has trouble speaking up, organizing his thoughts, and defending himself forcefully. When he is accused of something, he can't do much to clear himself. When he was accused of deliberately wetting his pants outside on a skating excursion and made to shiver in his own cold pee, he didn't speak up. And when he forgot his mitts and wasn't allowed to go back and get them – to teach him a lesson – and when the lesson turned out to be a severe case of frostbite he didn't complain before the damage was done. These are normal practices, I am told, of behaviour modification, and as object lessons they can be most effective, I am sure. I do think that the nature of the child must be considered, though, before one takes too harsh or arbitrary measures to teach him hard lessons. (Do I sound like a bleeding-heart mother?)

If you are considering sending your special child away to school, there are things to be considered other than the academic training of the staff. First, of course, check out the accreditation of the school, according to provincial standards. Find out whether graduates of the school progress to university or community college. Check dress, food, and health standards. What about church attendance: is it compulsory? Find out if there is a good athletic program. What kind of extracurricular activities are offered? Do the students have any kind of self-government; do they have any say in decisions? Check out the expectations the school has of the students' behaviour, and the methods of exacting that behaviour. And check out the staff's attitude to drugs. (I don't mean street drugs.)

Find out what kind of reputation the school has. If possible, talk to a few parents whose children have attended or are currently attending, and talk, too, to some members of the staff, other than the principal. Finally, take a look at the actual educational program of the school.

I had none of these luxuries or choices. I accepted the opportunity for Matt gratefully. I was not only grateful, I was blind and ultimately very frightened, as coerced as Matthew was. He must have sensed disaster from the very beginning, because his first nervous state requiring some prescribed relaxants occurred in the weeks preceding his departure for the school.

Well, no solutions, you'll find, are ever ideal.

The saga continues and it becomes hard to separate Matt's schooling from what happened next. There was a hiatus in his school career over the winter that he was seventeen and eighteen (in February), during which he had a nervous breakdown. Or a psychotic incident, as it is sometimes called now. An anxiety syndrome? Anyway, he withdrew from life for a while. As he was recovering and preparing to enter society again, the search began again for a suitable school. This time I knew there mustn't be too much pressure until he had fully recovered. He was still under twenty-one, so he was able to attend a Toronto School Board school for mentally retarded students. It served its purpose. I'm grateful for that, but it epitomized what happens to kids who are simply not expected to make any progress. They don't do anything, and neither does the staff.

These are harsh words, and I don't mean to be unfeeling or ungrateful — far from it. Teachers of m.r. kids are dedicated and patient, and besides, what would Matt and I have done without that school? But there is no incentive, no goal, and therefore no need or pressure of any kind to produce. These are functionally illiterate kids whose future when they turn twenty-one is to go to a sheltered workshop-training centre. They can't read, they can't write, they can't do simple arithmetic, and the teachers have stopped trying to teach them. They do more extracurricular activities than anything: bowling, yoga, movies. And they run errands for their teachers, picking up milk and cigarettes at the store, going to their homes to rake leaves or shovel snow, to help clean the storm windows — useful things like that. I can see it's a temptation on the part of teachers to let this happen. The kids have had a rough time. They have just about reached the end of the line as far as school is concerned. Why not let them take it easy?

But they're still educable. And there's still a lot they can learn.

The city school did, however, provide the necessary gentle re-entry to life that Matt needed the first year after his breakdown. The second year I felt he was marking time, making no progress. I found a school for younger children that provided tutorial remedial lessons in reading and paid extra for Matt to go there after his regular school. That helped a bit, but not much.

After the New Year, in his second year at the m.r. school, Matt moved into a group home. (Oh, there's a lot to say — we'll get to that, too.) His counsellor found a private school that she thought would really help him. We had an interview and the school director was willing to take Matt on the following fall – if I could come up with the very hefty fees. I managed to do that for two years and it was well worth them.

At last, at last, I had found someone who threw away labels, who judged each child for him- or herself, who knew that every child can learn. Simone Lebrun, the principal of Kohai Educational Centre, is a feisty French woman who doesn't believe "can't" is an answer. All children can learn, she maintains. It just takes longer for some. She uses patience and persistence and humour and endless repetition in her teaching methods. There's no real magic there, just effort.

The magic is in her attitude to her students. Each one is an individual, subject to the inexorable demands we make of ourselves. They are not allowed to hide behind labels or masks. They are free to be, they are expected to be, themselves. That's not easy, either. A lot of us never learn that.

CHAPTER SEVEN

CHURCH, CAMP, COMMUNITY

They can't stay in a cocoon forever. Sooner or later they have to face the world in the form of relatives, friends, community. Long before school starts they're learning their social skills. Or not, as the case may be.

The segregation starts early, with the natural selective process of friendship. Kids with problems often have more trouble making and keeping friends. If they're excitable and hyperactive, they can irritate and even wear out other kids. If they're badly coordinated and have trouble with balls and bicycles, let alone tree-climbing or model-building, then they lack the skills necessary to keep up with their peers. If they have trouble with their reading or with organizing their thoughts, then a lot of the board games like Monopoly, Life, Masterpiece, Dealer's Choice, and (heaven help us) Trivial Pursuit become home torture sets. And later on, if they've been lifted out of their neighbourhood school and put into a special-ed class with other problem kids, their range of friends is limited. The very fact of geographical distance from them can make accessibility a problem.

Yet after a certain age, social skills are more important than the ability to do long division. So it's a good thing to start early to help your child become an accepted, welcome member of the society he lives in. As might be expected, there are problems.

I'm trying to remember Matt's first experiences at church. We were a church-going family, peeling off members of the group as we went along, sending them to their different departments of

Sunday school. I taught Sunday school for about fourteen years, advancing with my children, until we arrived in Stratford and I graduated to choir where I got to stay in and hear the sermon every Sunday. From the very beginning Matthew was part of our family's Sunday activities.

There is a certain amount of cutting and snipping and fine-motor skill involved in Sunday school, not too much, not for a while. There, too, the gap gradually widens until a child can't keep up with his peers, and he begins to be put back with the work and the kids he can handle. It's a social problem; he knows he should be with the bigger kids. Then the teachers begin to be unable to cope with him. They hand out their little assignments, and here's this kid who can't read or write.

Sunday schools aren't required, as are school boards, to provide an education, however flawed, for everyone. I asked my current minister, Reverend Bob Wallace, about this, and he told me there is no policy statement in the United Church about handicapped people. Care and concern are an individual choice. The minister and the congregation set the standard in each community and decide how much or how little they will do.

In Matthew's case and in our church in Stratford there came a time, finally, when the Sunday-school teachers and the minister admitted there was no place for Matthew in the church. But they said they had an interesting program on records. Would he like to hear them? So every Sunday I would go off to choir and leave Matt at home with one of the kids to listen to his special recordings of Bible stories. The irony did not escape me. Before there was no room at the inn, Matt used to attend junior congregation; that is, he started out in church with the grown-ups, and after the children's story, would troop out with the little kids while everyone was singing the children's hymn. To do so he had to pass the choir, positioned at the stage-right side of the church. He always waved at me as he went by and I waved back, causing a ripple of appreciation from the assembly. He really was a cute kid. I wonder if anyone in the congregation missed him?

After we moved to Toronto (he was fourteen by that time) Matthew attended adult church with me. He may be bored with a lot of what goes on in church, but he gets practice in numbers, finding his way around the hymn-book, and he knows how to behave. He's very good at coffee time, and moves around and talks to more people and remembers more names than I do.

But the time had come for him to join the church and I was worried about confirmation classes. If confirmation training was going to be more schoolwork and essays, then he certainly couldn't go through the classes with kids his own age. I phoned the minister, Donald Henderson, to discuss it with him. It turned out he was planning group discussions that year, no paperwork, or so he said. The decision may have been taken when I told him about Matthew. We were new in the congregation so Mr. Henderson took some time to find out a little of Matt's and my background, and he used his information well and daringly.

The very first night when the young people began to probe the profundities of life and death, and wondered how and if they would ever be able to cope, the minister singled out Matt and asked him to talk about his father's death. None of the other kids had suffered the death of anyone close to them, let alone a father, so Matt had information and experience far beyond theirs. They listened respectfully to what he had to say. He was not only part of the group, he was a valuable contributing member. Later I learned that Mr. Henderson had briefed the other kids, gently warning them to be patient if Matt was a little slow in his expression. Matt can be very simple and powerful, however, and once encouraged, he gained confidence with the group. So he joined the church, and it meant a lot to him. He had tears in his eyes that Palm Sunday at his confirmation. So did I.

He still has terrible trouble finding the hymns fast enough. He has a monotone voice; his words come in at least a beat behind anyone else's because of his lack of reading skill; and he still gets bored; but he likes to go to church with me. He likes the annual dinner and the Christmas party and the congregational picnic and the variety night, and he likes coffee time, and that's part of what fellowship is all about. It's certainly what social skills are all about.

Some parents, depending on the degree of their child's handicap, tend to hide the kid at home, or send him off to segregated activities. I think it's essential to accept the child for what he is, and then to be proud of him for what he can accomplish. I have often acted as buffer, interpreter, and even censor for Matt in a casual encounter. He is so open he has trouble differentiating between strangers, acquaintances, and friends, and he tends to tell people more than they care to know about whatever is uppermost in his mind. He has to be reminded about what is appropriate behaviour. At least he wants to talk.

I mentioned that Matt began swimming lessons at a very early age. We belonged to a winter club in Winnipeg with very good facilities, so it was easy to arrange group lessons with other little friends. He tried ice-skating, too. He was on bob skates for the longest time, but he could con anyone into taking him around the ice. A special child, when he is young, is often singled out and cherished more than a normal one by kindly people. Some of them are consciously kind, some of their attitudes are patronizing; but others are genuinely caring. Most are protective.

In the early spring after we had moved into a big old house in Winnipeg, I was busy painting one of the bedrooms and asked the girls to watch Matt outside while I finished. Well, he got away from them. I didn't know that though until a week later when I was talking to a woman at the winter club where Matt swam with her little girl. This woman told me that she had been coming out of her mother's house a block away from ours when she heard a terrible racket and saw Matt walking down the middle of the street pulling his noisy red tin wagon behind him, happy as a tick. She didn't call out because he was in the middle of an intersection and she knew he would stop when he heard his name. So she went to meet him at the corner, and called him from there. Sure enough, he stopped. My friend brought Matt over to the sidewalk, led him back to his side of the street, and sent him home. She didn't even know where we had moved to. We were so new in the neighbourhood, having just moved in over the New Year, that no one else would have recognized Matt. You see, there really are guardian angels. There is also such a thing as community, and while it's important to everyone, it's especially important to the damaged in our society. I think the measure of a society's progress lies as much in its treatment of the maimed, the halt, the crippled, the blind, the old — whoever cannot make it on their own — as it does in the contents of its galleries, museums, theatres, and concert halls.

Matthew joined a scout troop after we moved to Toronto. Again, somehow, the church we attended in Stratford couldn't quite manage to take him in, but this scout troop did and it was a happy, productive association for him for two years. He even won a prize for the most improvement in a year! Prizes are rare for l.d. kids and they mean a lot when they come.

Camp is another story. John had profited so by the wonderful summer camp that he attended, and we were so busy in Stratford in the summer, that it seemed like a good idea to send Matt to summer camp, if we could find one. I asked Dr. Bruno Morawetz, John's camp director, to meet Matt to see whether he thought the boy could handle camp life. Not at his camp, Morawetz thought, after assessing Matt carefully. However, I found out about a Y in Toronto that was planning a camp for l.d. kids for the first time.

As you might expect, there was a staff member at that Y who had an l.d. kid himself, and who managed to push the idea onto the rest of the organizers.

The camp had not been well-attended for the previous few years, so there were space and time to spare for the experiment. I enrolled Matt and duplicated all the equipment I'd had to buy for John: groundsheet, campfire cooking utensils, and so on. I labelled all his clothes, bought a new bar of floating soap, knowing full well it would never be touched, and sent him off. I also had to buy tranquillizers.

These were for me, prescribed by my doctor. The old familiar ulcer was still eating holes in my stomach, though I had it pretty well under control – that is, until Matt went away to camp. Worry?! That's when I realized how structured and secure I had made Matthew's life. Lots of things were easy for him to do because they were made so possible for him. How would it be when he went to camp and these things were no longer easy? Would he be able to cope? Would he survive?

Lots of mothers worry when their kids go off to camp. I did my share of fussing when John went each year. I preferred not to hear about jumping off Diving Rock and bears attacking their tumps and exciting stories like that. With a special child the anxiety is worse. I couldn't help it. It's one of the things mothers are not supposed to do with their special one, feel that they are the only ones who can understand him, the only ones who care, the only ones who can deal with him. This attitude, carried to extremes, can ruin a mother's (and a father's) life and cripple the kid for life as well. You see old l.d. or m.r. people living with even older parents, and you wonder what's going to happen to them when their parents die. It's a terrible and easy temptation to be the buffer and the protector always, but you can't do that. That was my first painful brush with this hard lesson. There was more to learn, but that would come in good time.

Anyway, there I was taking tranquillizers, having trouble sleeping, waking up in the night and worrying about Matthew. Apart from all that, I really missed him. He was our golden boy, our court jester, our sunshine kid. I can still see him bobbing up and down in the pool (we put a swimming pool in because we couldn't get away; summer was our busiest time in Stratford). The smile never left his face. It's a wonder he didn't have chlorine stains on his teeth. He used to spend eight or nine hours a day in the water. I could barely lure him out to the patio to eat a sandwich. The first few days his nose would be so burned it was one massive peel, but he put a hat on his head (he was a hat man, too) and went on bobbing. There was no doubt he was confident in the water. That was one thing I wasn't worried about.

Well, we drove up to visit both the boys. Their camps were not far apart. We had seen John in action before, so we didn't stay long. Then we went over to another lake and found Matt at his camp. His teeth were already green; he'd lost his toothbrush the first day. I gave him mine. He was dirty. But he really was okay. Even I could see that.

The camp director, the one with the l.d. kid of his own, thanked us for sending Matthew to camp. He said the experiment worked because of him! Matt was so well-adjusted, so happy, that he became the focus for all the activities. If Matt went along with something, then the counsellors knew it would work. In fact, they almost ruined Matt's holiday, the director said, because they had put him in a tent with the worst behaviour problem in the camp, hoping some of Matt's placidity and good cheer would rub off on him. Instead, the kid had beat up on Matt, so they were finally separated.

When Bruno Morawetz sent his report from Camp Ponacka about John that summer, he reported on Matt, too. He actually went over to Matt's camp to see how he was getting along! I've never forgotten that.

Anyway, Matt's first camping experience was a success. I stopped taking the tranquillizers as soon as he came home. The only annoyance we had to get over was a really horrendous collection of zits on his face. He hadn't washed his face for three weeks. We were swimming in a friend's pool before he had recovered from this oil attack, and the woman looked sharply at Matt as he was about to jump into her clean water. "Is that impetigo?" she asked. "No, it's zits," said Matt, and jumped in. He liked pools better than lakes.

The Y experiment was not repeated the following year; they had a full enrollment of normal kids, so the l.d. campers were cut out. But my contact sent me a brochure about a new camp designed especially for l.d. kids. The pamphlet was in the mail with my sympathy cards. I dropped a note to the director asking for information but warning him that as a brand-new widow I didn't have much money. He wrote back and said that scholarships were available. Thus began a relationship that was initially extremely valuable for Matthew, and for which I was extremely grateful. The fact that it ended so disastrously couldn't be helped, I guess.

Matt went off to a summer camp that not only taught him a lot, but also taught me a lot about my son over the several years that he attended. I learned, for example, he has a will, determination, persistence, and courage beyond what anyone would expect in such a gentle, easy-going boy. The year he and his team walked and camped on the Bruce Trail, he must have walked at least a mile a day on his knees, he fell down so much. But the scrapes and bruises were nothing to the blisters he developed on his feet. He did not complain about them, however, and no one discovered them until they were back in home camp. Other kids with far less cause were whining, I was told, but not Matt. He picked up an infection one summer and came home with boils the size of quarters on his back, and suffered the hot compresses (to bring out the infection) with clenched fists and grimaces but no tears.

He could make other kids laugh. He always surprises people with his sense of humour. They don't expect the wit he can exhibit, and do a sharp double-take wondering whether he intended to make a joke, or whether he really didn't know what he was saying. He really knows what he's saying.

He could always talk to girls, and surprised his camp counsellors and the other boys by somehow walking off with the girls on the work parties.

He has no aptitude whatsoever for manual labour. And he wouldn't be much better as a file clerk. His face and his personality are his fortune, but I still have no idea what he's going to do with his life. But he's doing it, and he has already had an influence on other people. He has an amazing ability to grapple people to his soul with their devotion to his well-being and future.

The camp director seemed to be no exception. When I went to pick up Matt on the last day of camp, I had an interview with the young man. His first words to me were, "Matt will never be a university graduate." I certainly knew that. But, the man said, Matt had "potential" and he wasn't going to let go of him. Nor did he, for a long time. He used to phone during the year, including on Christmas Day, to check up on Matt and to wish him well. He really watched over my son and came to visit us with his wife, both in Stratford and in Toronto after we moved there. He became like a big brother to Matthew, and since I had no man to consult about Matt's future, and no role model (as they say) for Matt to pattern himself after, this young man became our mentor and our ideal. And as I said earlier, it was on his advice and by his good graces that he got Matt into the special school he had started. Somewhere along the way it turned out not to be the right thing, but I am still grateful for all he did for Matthew. He was our friend.

For the moment, that's irrelevant to the factors you may want to consider before you send your l.d. child to camp. First of all, of course, the child's own particular needs and situation must be evaluated. If he's really tired and tense from the pressure of school, he may need an unpressured holiday at home. But if the other kids on the street are away and there's no one to play with, or if the parents are both extremely busy and can't give him much time and attention, or if he really needs some gross-motor training, then camp might be very good for him.

It's hard to keep a kid productively occupied all summer, especially if he has trouble entertaining himself. Television is not the answer, not for the entire summer anyway. Our swimming pool helped a lot, and helped Matt make friends, too. It's hard to ostracize a kid with a pool. Water is a great leveller. We used to have a lot of pool parties, both for actors and neighbours, and Matt was never excluded from any water games. But even pools pall, especially if the weather is less than ideal. So camp may be a welcome change in the middle of the summer.

It's important to check out the accreditation of a camp, just as with a school. Make sure that the camp you're considering is a member of the provincial camping association. Check out what kind of medical facilities it has, not only within the camp itself (resident doctor or nurse?), but also within a fairly short driving range (i.e., the nearest hospital).

One of the reasons John's camp director thought that his camp would be unsuitable for Matthew was that his camp activities were highly competitive. This is not a good idea for l.d. kids. Competitions always involve prizes to be won and achievement to be recognized. If someone wins, that means that someone loses. That's the last thing an l.d. kid needs on his vacation – another chance to fail. That's just more pressure, pressure he doesn't need.

Some kids don't need a special camp; give them maybe an extra year to mature (and it's not a great idea to send any child away to camp before he's seven or eight years old) and they may do just fine at a "normal" camp.

As for his dressing, sorting, and packing ability, don't worry about it. I never knew any kid who wore more than the top layer of clothes in his bag. If Matt survived his zits, your kid can survive dirty clothes, green teeth, uncombed hair, all that. Camp is the first out-of-the-nest experience most kids will have, and it's particularly valuable for a special child whom you may have been protecting too much. It will be good for both of you!

Friends are what you need a lot of when you have a brain-damaged child, and even more so when the child loses his father. There were other resources in the community that provided Matt with such friendships. The Big Brothers organization, with its generous men who reach out to help fatherless boys, meant a lot to Matt and me. In Stratford we had just a taste of the kind of sharing such men do from a man who brought his own daughter along on most excursions, thus giving thirteen-year-old Matt a welcome opportunity to talk to a girl. Then in Toronto, although there was a huge waiting list for brothers, Matt shot to the top of the list because of his disability and gained one of his best friends. Barry

Cranstoun stayed with Matt long after the sixteen-year-old cut-off date and became a real friend of the family. In an unofficial way he became John's Big Brother, too.

The YMCA remains one of the best resources in any community. You often don't know where one kind of help begins and another leaves off with the Y. For two summers the Y "hired" Matthew as a volunteer counsellor to help with day-camp kids, and then paid him (a nominal amount) for a third summer to continue. It wasn't really the right work for Matthew to do, but the Y made allowances for his shortcomings, thus helping him as well as his charges.

One thing I wish the Y could provide for Matthew, and young adults like him, is some sort of phys-ed program. Again, he's out of sync with his age group. His coordination and his ability to follow directions are not as good as those of normal young men his age. I wish there were some way he could get more exercise — group exercise, that is.

But there are other resources in the community, in any community, and you will find them in yours if you seek them out. Minimally brain-damaged young people may be able to hang out with their peers, but people like Matthew who have a greater assortment of problems or who, also like Matthew, lack a group of close friends with whom they have grown up may find they don't have much to do on a Friday night. In Toronto there is a Friday Night Club, run especially for m.r. people and providing a variety of activities and social programs for young adults who have no other place to go. There are movies, bingo, dances, and so on, and young people from all over the city go to this club. If there isn't one where you live, it wouldn't take too much effort to organize it through a local church or Y or some other community organization.

Perhaps I have become more aware of my dependency upon the community and the resources and services it has to offer because of my widowhood. Since there were things I wasn't able to do all by myself, I had to learn to lean on other people. For example, I will never forget my gratitude to the two family friends who in two successive years each took Matt to a scouts' father-and-son banquet. And there were things I couldn't afford to do for Matt by myself, so I gratefully accepted aid from various sources to enrich his life and further his development. One of my friends gave Matt an extra month at summer camp when I had surgery and couldn't make a home for him until I had recovered. Another friend gave him two winter weekends cross-country skiing at a reunion with his summer campers. Relatives have taken him in when I had to go away and had no one to leave him with. Men friends have counselled him in ways that I could not. I am deeply appreciative for the support of my friends. But sometimes one does run out of resources, both financial and spiritual.

When one does, it might be wise to consider joining a parent support group. If you can't find one in your community, either within your church or Y or community club, then form one yourself. It can be a tiny, loosely knit association, easy to fit in anyone's living room, just a few anxious parents who need a little comfort and reassurance in what they often view as a very lonely, private struggle for survival. You don't have to be movers and shakers. You don't have to make any great political statements. It may be enough just to discuss a few practical solutions to your most immediate daily problems. Whatever gets you through the day. Some days you need it as much as your child does.

While personal friends are valuable and to be prized, many handicapped people find care-givers in the community. (See circle groups, page 153.) Right now, Matt has a "volunteer" that he goes to the movies with. There are various types of Friends (of Schizophrenics, of the Mentally Handicapped, of Ex-Mental Patients, of Ex-Prisoners, and so on) whose volunteer services are the development of a one-to-one relationship with someone who needs a friend. Also an adviser, a buddy, a helper, a cheering section. Well, what do friends do? Be sure to make enquiries in your community and find out if an organization of "friends" exists. There is, for example, an association called People First, with groups springing up across Canada. They got their name from a young woman in the United States who protested the label *retarded* for their new self-advocacy group.

"We want to be seen as people first," she said. And so they are, and other people in our communities recognize that fact, proclaiming and ensuring their own humanity by helping other human beings.

This is what I mean when I talk about community, the network of support and caring, both public and private, that goes on all around you and is ready to reach out and enfold you, both you and your child. It's a very real comfort to any parent of a special child to know that it's there.

CHAPTER EIGHT

THE SINGLE PARENT

Bereavement in a family can cause problems and pain for any member of it, let alone for a special child. The danger of long-lasting emotional problems increases when the child is already struggling with his own insecurity and fear of failure. If ever there was a time when the other members of the family have to rally round and support each other it must be when there is a death or divorce in their midst. The fact of death and the inevitable changes that the death will force within the family group must be faced head-on. Each member of the family, of course, must go through the grief process. The special child may have to have extra help to get through it.

Matthew's father died suddenly when Matt was twelve years old. I have described something of the effects of my husband's death in another book; the focus in this one will be on Matt and on the learning-disabled child.

A kind of madness grips anyone who encounters death, especially perhaps sudden death. Matthew was sitting in a chair close to his father when Bill fell forward onto the coffee table, dropping his glass on the floor. For days afterward, Matt talked about that glass, wondering what had happened to it. The detail, seemingly irrelevant, stuck in his mind; it must have seemed to him the proof that his father was dead and gone. At the moment of the event, as I was attempting artificial resuscitation and our dinner guest was calling a doctor, Matt went down to the recreation room where

John was watching television and told his brother, "Dad's dead." He knew before anyone. He *knew*.

After the funeral we spent an extra day together before we parted. The children went their separate ways to school and I — I can't remember what I did. Matt's special-ed teacher required an impossible response from his schoolmates. She told them of his father's death and charged them to treat Matt normally in spite of it, not to make a fuss about it with him. Not knowing how to handle this injunction, they solved their problem by not speaking to Matt at all — no help. The prime need is to talk about the death, to keep reliving the incredulous shock, surprise, and fear associated with it until it's possible, if not to understand it, at least to begin to come to terms with it.

It happened that our evening game at that time was a new one I had ordered recently from an educational toy catalogue. Played like Fish, it was a language-training game of homonyms. Words like *pear* and *pair*, when mated, had to be used in sentences before the set could be claimed. Trying to keep life as normal as possible for Matt, I continued to play the game with him each night. As it turned out, it gave him an opportunity to go over and over in his mind what had happened to his father. Every sentence he framed had something to do with death, dying, graves, cemeteries, and other images he held or fears he harboured. The game gave him the detachment and distance he needed to give utterance to his feelings in an acceptable way. It was enormously helpful.

I saved the sympathy cards and letters till evening when everyone was home and we could share them. I tried to keep the doors of communication open between the children and me, but I'm not sure how well I succeeded. Each of us had his or her own private battlefield of pain to struggle through. I know the children gave me as much as or more help than I gave them, hugging me, talking to me, helping me. Matt walked with me, leaving his playmates to catch up and accompany me on the Sunday walks I continued to try to take (for a while) without my husband. And Matt left his seat at the dinner table when he could see weather warnings in me, and came to pat my hand or hug me. He was always enormously sensitive to other people's feelings, and not solely those of his immediate family.

The summer immediately following my husband's death was a

difficult time for all of us, adjusting as we were to life without father. But it was more than that. We all had to learn to trust in life again. A sudden death makes you realize how fleeting life can be, and how uncertain. I guess that's what was bothering Matthew when he went to visit friends at their lake. He had been there for five days, and I was coming down to spend the weekend with them.

The morning of my expected arrival, Matt refused to go down to the beach with his two buddies. Instead, he hung around the cottage until I arrived. It wasn't just that he was eager to see me after an absence of only five days. Something else was bothering him. Once I arrived, he said a quick hi and joined his pals. The weekend passed very pleasantly. When I was preparing to leave, however, on the Sunday night, Matt came to me in tears, asking me not to go. I said I had to, so Matt decided he wanted to go with me. It finally came out that he was worried about my driving on the highway. What if something happened to me? The best thing to do, he figured, was to go with me and keep an eye on me. He came home with me, spent a couple of days quietly in the house, sticking close. Then when he was assured that I wasn't going to do anything foolish like die on him, he agreed to go back to the lake with his friends.

Whenever Matt or I wanted to talk about his father over the succeeding years, we have been assured of a sympathetic audience in each other. I keep trying to be open with him about all his problems, facing them squarely and discussing them. It helps to pull them out in the open. You give a problem additional strength if you hide it and refuse to acknowledge it, I think. So, in dealing with our bereavement, we have been able to look each other in the eyes and say, "It's hell, isn't it?" whenever either of us has been feeling particularly down. "Yes, it is," the other one will answer fervently. That helps, the simple fact that someone else shares your anguish and sense of loss.

One time I was walking past Matt's room when he was playing a record; George Harrison was singing "My Sweet Lord."

"My sweet Lord," I heard Matthew say, "why did you take my Dad?" So I stopped and asked if I could come in, then said, "Do you want to talk about it?" and we did. The pain and the questions keep surfacing and they must be dealt with. There are no answers, of course, but it helps to share what we have—in our case, fortunately, a belief in some kind of afterlife. We put such a bright, unreal face on bereavement, it's sometimes a comfort to let go, to admit to someone else that we still feel "rotten" about it, as Matt would say.

A handicapped person who lacks communication skills will find it more difficult to let go like this. They have to be helped to put their feelings into words (so do most adult men). Go ahead and put words into his mouth. Soon he'll get the idea and add a few of his own—not many, perhaps, but to the point. It hurts. It still hurts. It's a deep pain. During the relatively few seizures Matt has had in his life (that's the next chapter), when he calls out from the unconscious depths of his being, his cries are for his father.

And yet I maintain that Matt has dealt with his mourning, that his grief-work is completed. I believe this because I have seen and heard how he helps other people, knowing more than they do, and serene in his confidence to guide them on a path he has walked himself. These were young people Matthew met during his breakdown whom he talked to and helped. As any person who has been bereaved will tell you, "You have to have been there yourself." Matt has been there.

The separation imposed by divorce has something of the same far-reaching and damaging effect on a special child. He has been deprived, usually of his father, a key link in his support system that threatens his equilibrium when it is withdrawn. The inadequacies a special child faces are bad enough without this terrible hole in his heart. I have told the story elsewhere (but it bears repeating) of a playmate of Matt's who taunted him with the call, "Nyah, Nyah, I'm better than you because I have a father and you don't." It's another of life's unanswerable inequities that this child had to suffer. And divorce imposes it just as harshly as death does.

So it becomes important to assure your special child of his continuing value to the family, of your need for each other, of your never-ending support even though his father is gone from his life, or effectively removed from daily contact with him, as in the case of divorce or separation. A special child will often suffer the deprivation of one or other of the parents more than the other "normal" children involved, so an attempt must be made to find some sort of compensation or substitute. I have already talked about the value and importance of the Big Brothers program to a special child. It is certainly worth pursuing.

The phrase "male role model" is such a cliché, too glib to be trusted, that we tend to dismiss it. But the need for such a model becomes especially apparent when there is a lonely l.d. boy in your house. If I sound as if I'm addressing mothers directly here, you're right. There are more widows than widowers, and divorced mothers still get custody of the children more often than the fathers, so it is a natural assumption on my part, as is the assumption, based on statistical evidence, that the damaged child is male. Counsellors, camp directors, and educators have usually been able to tell that Matthew had very few men in his life, that he was, by and large, raised by a woman, and in female company much of his time. Mothers like me who face this problem will do well to seek out male help to solve it. If you have a brother or a brother-in-law, a neighbour, a cousin, or a close friend of the family who can fill this role, then be grateful and hang on to him for he will do your child a world of good and ease the load for you, too.

If you are fortunate enough to have a faith, then it will help you and your children face death with some measure of comfort. But you can't shove something at your kids you don't believe yourself. They'll spot your insincerity at once. Honest doubt is okay, though. None of us knows for certain whether there is an afterlife. As one woman put it to me, "I'd rather go through life behaving as if there is another life and find out I was right than slug through as if there weren't and find out I was wrong." Matthew seems to have a serene assurance about his father's whereabouts. He told me of a chance encounter one day. He met a young woman in our apartment pool and had a suddenly significant conversation. Her father had recently died, he discovered, and he told her his was dead, too. "But he's in heaven," he said to the girl, "and so is your dad, if he lived a good life."

Critics have dumped on *Jonathan Livingston Seagull* for its kitschy brand of religion, if you can call it that, but the story has a simple appeal that is comforting and easy to understand. When it first came out I read it aloud to Matt, and it gave us a chance to discuss the afterlife together. (I used it again later when my mother died.) The idea of progressing through increasingly difficult problems or assignments is a good one for l.d. kids to think about, too (and for their parents). We all have barriers we must break through. As quickly as we solve one problem, another one pops up. So I find *Seagull* a useful resource book, and you may, too.

There are other, more conventional books on helping your children deal with bereavement, and I've included some in the bibliography. As important as it is to help the entire family go through effective grief-work, it's even more important for a special child to be helped through it. Again, though, there may be blessings in disguise. I have already described our minister's daring use of Matt's personal encounter with bereavement in his confirmation classes, and the reinforcement it gave Matt. Matt's other relationships have often been coloured by this special knowledge of his, too. And he has helped me through many bad times, with comfort and hugs.

The American psychologist Virginia Satir has for several years been stressing the importance of hugs. You need four a day, according to Satir, for survival; eight a day for maintenance; and twelve a day for growth. Few people get that many, but if you have a loving, dependent child like Matthew in your house, you have a better guarantee! The support is mutual: both hugger and huggee benefit. And you can take a lesson from your l.d. child and extend your hugs to the other members of the family. We all need them.

When there is a death in the family, the continuing health of the survivors depends upon an assurance of the continuity of the family and of normal family life. The structured environment you may have set up for your special child will prove to be valuable to all of you at the time of bereavement. At least there is a routine you can count on to carry you through, some ordinary but tangible reassurance that life does, indeed, go on, and that all of you can keep on living and developing despite this loss in your lives.

There are four times as many widows as there are widowers, and there are seven times as many divorcées as there are widows. These are statistics that would seem to justify my concentration on the widow or divorcée with a handicapped child. But statistics and life being what they are, I am aware that there are widowers and divorcés out there who also carry the burden of a special child in their loneliness. Often it's harder for them, and for the child, especially a younger child. Housekeepers are hard enough to find and pay for; they are especially so if you need someone with the skills required to handle the problems of a brain-injured child. Too often, the child must sink or swim in such a situation. Usually, he sinks. I'm not saying that mothers are indispensable, but they are more available – or used to be, before the double-income family became so common. Time was when a man would remarry quickly to replace the domestic pattern and the services he and his children needed. But in these times, women are not as ready to take on the cares of a ready-made family. Other careers are open to them.

Each case is so individual, as are the solutions, that I hesitate to offer anything with authority. Grandmothers and aunts and saintly neighbours have been known to come to the rescue, but you can't count on them. Of course, you can't count on anything these days, so you can't let that bother you too much. In my trusting way I want to assure you: nature abhors a vacuum.

Case in point: my children were left quite early in their lives with only one living grandparent. But my husband's spinster aunt surprised us all by marrying on her retirement, thus providing us with a wonderful pair of grandparent surrogates. Great-uncle Jim and Great-aunt Nell were classics, complete with homemade cookies, humbugs in the pocket (Jim), admiring attendance at music festivals and church concerts, and invitations to movies and basketball games, as well as staggering meals.

Surely somewhere can be found extra compassion and help for special cases in need. If this care is not available, then a damaged child will surely suffer further damage. You don't have to read Gothic novels to see what happens to the lonely, neglected children of bereaved or single fathers. It's still happening.

People keep telling you that you're not alone, that there are community facilities now and support systems that you can plug into to help your learning-disabled or handicapped child. But if you are widowed or divorced, you can't help but feel alone – and you are. It's not a unique problem these days, however, what with the high incidence of divorce.

Various interviewing officials are learning to be more tactful when they make their enquiries about marital status. Most children learn to handle the questions with poise. The poise can be deceptive, though. Just because they can handle the question doesn't mean they have absorbed the hard lesson contained in it. Sometimes, in the case of divorce, a child feels more deprived and discriminated against than in the case of bereavement. As one divorced woman said to me, "At least you know where your husband is!" The same fact bears its harsh comfort for the child whose parent dies. It usually wasn't the intention of his father to die. But what can the child say, how can he justify or protect himself against the fact of his father's or mother's departure from the household? It's another example to the child of his own failure, this inability to hang onto both his parents. You'll have to watch for signs that the child in some way blames himself for the divorce or separation, and hasten to assure him that it was not his fault. Then, if you think he still needs it, seek professional help to reassure him further. As I say, help is available.

All the events of life, sad or happy, small or large, unimportant or traumatic, become significant obstacles to be dealt with, overcome, absorbed, or coped with when you have a special child. Perhaps it will make you more aware of your other children's difficulties and needs, and give you the idea that they need help, too, to cope with their eventful lives.

Humour helps a lot. On Easter Sunday seven years after Bill's death, all the kids were with me. They came to meet me at my bedroom door when I got up that morning, singing as rehearsed, "Happy anniversary to you." The anniversary we were celebrating was their father's death; he died on Easter Sunday. They told me they figured I was strong enough to take it by that time. Matthew, of course, joined in the singing. So we had our hot cross buns that morning and also a chat about memorial societies, as I remember. This may sound callous but it wasn't. We had a warm, hearty conversation, with lots of black humour, to be sure, but lots of love, too.

Love and laughter. It's possible to achieve them even, or especially, when things look blackest. All your children can benefit by them. The question is, who is teaching whom?

CHAPTER NINE

EPILEPSY

What is epilepsy? Epilepsy is a disorder involving sudden bursts of electrical energy in the brain. These discharges cause seizures which can take many forms, from violent jerking, to strange movements, sensation, behaviour, perception, and sometimes loss of consciousness. Epilepsy can begin in anyone, at any age. The disorder is the result of some interruption in the normal activity of the brain. Contributing factors may be a head injury, a chemical imbalance, a birth trauma. Frequently the cause cannot be discovered. (from an information booklet published by the Epilepsy Association)

Matthew had his second seizure when he was twelve and a half years old.

I heard a rhythmical thumping on the wall of his bedroom, which was under mine, early one morning and went to investigate. The worst was over by the time I got to him but his arm was still twitching involuntarily. It had been his arm knocking against the wall that had wakened me. His eyes were glazed; he did not respond to questions; his left arm and left leg were dragging; he had dirtied himself. I was terrified. Fortunately, the public health nurse was living with us that fall. I called her to take a look at Matthew while I phoned the doctor. Thus began a long, strange day, and a long, strange week.

After a brief check-in at the Stratford General Hospital, I ended up following an ambulance with Matthew in it to the War Memorial

Children's Hospital in London, Ontario. And so we began to find out something about epilepsy.

I like to say now that Matt is mildly epileptic, but that's like saying someone is slightly pregnant: you either are or you aren't. Matthew was fortunate (I keep counting our blessings) that he had never had a recurrence of the convulsion he had had in the incubator when he was three days old. Thus, he had spent his childhood without drugs. I understand that the anticonvulsant drugs, while effective in curbing seizures, may also have some detrimental side effects over the long term, and that these side effects can affect the growth of the skeleton (especially the teeth and gums) and the normal development of the body in a growing child. I guess I'm such a grasshopper in the sunshine, it never occurred to me that Matt might ever have another convulsion. I took him to a doctor in Toronto several years later to enquire about his future, and the man looked at me as if I were a hopeless idiot when I told him Matt had had a convulsion when he was three days old. That settled everything, he said. Though there were twelve intervening years between seizures, Matt was definitely an epileptic, he said.

Once an epileptic, always an epileptic. So we had better call a spade a spade and learn as much as we can about a condition that seems to attract a lot of awe, fear, and superstition, to say nothing of prejudice.

Julius Caesar was an epileptic. So were artist Vincent Van Gogh, writers Charles Dickens, Lord Byron, and Dostoevsky, musicians Handel, Beethoven, and Tchaikovsky, and so was and is actors Michael Wilding and John Considine. And it's a good thing, because they help give epilepsy a good name, and it needs one. Everyone probably has in his mind a lurid picture of a poor soul writhing on the ground and foaming at the mouth in the grip of a convulsion. "Fits," they used to be called, and people who suffered from them used to be feared, and frequently ostracized. Some ancient civilizations considered epileptics to be possessed by a god, but our civilization is reluctant to give them a driving licence. Discrimination is a serious problem. Matt has suffered from it.

But I didn't know all this that cool day in October when I drove behind the ambulance to London. All I knew was that I was very, very frightened for my son. At the hospital he was hustled off to bed. He had a terrible headache and just wanted to sleep. (I gather that the residual effect of a seizure must be something like a hangover.) I talked to a number of doctors, giving birth history and background (anyone with a special child becomes awfully good at this). I spent the next week driving back and forth from Stratford to London, while Matt was under observation.

Matt had an EEG and his brain waves were pretty good, according to the doctor, but he wanted to keep watching him for a bit. And then he asked permission to hold Matt over till his Thursday class because he wanted to introduce my son to his young psychiatrists and interns, because, he said, they so seldom saw a child with a problem who had been so well handled, who was functioning to the best of his ability, who was so well adjusted, and such an outstanding personality (I quote from my diary record of the man's description of Matt). The doctor concluded then that I had done "all the right things." That's great comfort to give a parent of a problem child. One is assailed by doubt all the time.

So I spent the week playing Monopoly with Matt and his roommate and reading to him. Matt conducted his clinic with the doctors, and handled himself beautifully. I said nothing, just sat and listened. A young doctor introduced him and asked him questions, then invited questions from the floor. Matt fielded them all, as poised and straightforward as if he did that sort of thing every day. He discussed his relationship with his siblings, with me, with his peers, and acknowledged his "problem" openly. I was very proud of him.

Then we had to start living with drugs. The London doctor had put Matt on phenobarbital as an anticonvulsant and asked me to monitor Matt's reaction to the drug. It was terrible, I reported. The kid was fighting his way out of a paper bag every morning. He wasn't my bright, sunny Matthew any more. So the phenobarb was reduced to a low dosage that allowed Matt to function well, and we more or less forgot about it, except to remember to take it. I, in my blind optimism, assumed the problem was solved. It still didn't occur to me to classify Matthew as an epileptic. That just shows how naïve I am.

So, in the fullness of time, we moved to Toronto. The seizure had become in my mind simply a manifestation of puberty, a changing time for Matthew, but a milestone not to be repeated.

Liz had her own place in Toronto while she went to university, but she and Kate (both out of the nest by the time I left Stratford) still used my place as a headquarters. Liz had a Christmas party here the first year and served hot apple cider — spiked with vodka. Matthew didn't know about the vodka and drank quite a lot of the cider. The next morning, in the twilight zone between sleeping and waking, Matthew had the third convulsion of his life.

It wasn't as bad as the first (second) one, though of course it was frightening to me. The weekend between Christmas and New Year's is no time to hustle off to hospital. I called the doctor with whom I had established contact in the city (a neurological pediatrician) and she assured me of his swift recovery — and, indeed, it was faster than the first time (second time). In the New Year, Matt had another EEG, and everything seemed normal. He continued on his low dosage of phenobarb.

When he started at his boarding school, of course, the examinations began again. I had to supply a complete history, and Matt was given a complete physical, in the course of which the school doctor found that he had very little phenobarbital in his blood stream, a fact he found disturbing. He thought that the danger of convulsions was greater because of this low dosage, so he increased it, a fact I found disturbing. It seemed to me that Matthew was back in his paper bag. The drug slowed all his reactions. It was hard enough for him to learn things with all those short circuits in his brain impeding his progress, without having to fight a drug as well. But I was helpless to protest because Matthew was out of my jurisdiction. He was living at the boarding school, coming home on weekends when he could manage it, when he was granted leave.

I checked with the neurological pediatrician when Matt came home for Christmas that year, and expressed my worries about the phenobarb. She advised me to wait until I had him with me and then to cut off the drug entirely and see what happened, if, that is, he'd had no further convulsions by that time. So that summer I rented a cottage and took Matt away with me for a holiday and a cooking course. I bought all the mixes and kits I could find, from Aunt Jemima's Pancake Mix to Chef Boy-ar-dee's Pizza Mix to Hamburger Helper, and sacrificed three pounds (gain!) in the interests of Matt's learning to cook. And I cut him off the phenobarbital.

It was a lovely holiday. Matt learned something about cooking; we both relaxed (though I had to take my typewriter with me and keep working), and the paper bag gradually lifted off his head.

He went away to camp the next month, and the counsellors, many of them the same people who taught him at his boarding school in the winter, were impressed with his sharpness. He was functioning, as they say, very well.

The previous fall, in fear of the unknown and the thought of leaving home, Matthew had been very uptight about going away to boarding school. This fall, by contrast, he was looking forward to it. He was bright and eager; he knew what he was doing; he was planning on a very good year. And then at the end of September, in the twilight zone between sleeping and waking, he had another seizure, a bad one. They saved his life, pulled his tongue out of his throat, and slapped him back on the phenobarb. He came home for the weekend that evening, unhappy, upset, uptight, calling himself a failure, worried about his future, wondering what his father would think of him, and jealous of his brother, who was home to celebrate his birthday. That was the beginning of a countdown that led to the next major upset of Matt's life. His life, in fact, reads like a really tacky soap opera. Tune in for the next depressing instalment!

But we're still talking about his seizures.

What happened in the following year or so deserves another chapter. I think Matthew had one brief flurry and a memory lapse that may or may not have been part of his epileptic history (everything is). The one really positive discovery that emerged from his sojourn in the Clarke Institute was the substitution of Dilantin for the phenobarb he had been taking. As far as I could see, the Dilantin did not have those mind-numbing side effects. As he recovered from his other problems, Matt seemed to me to be functioning better. However, we knew now that he couldn't drink.

Well, we knew that, didn't we? We had already discovered that phenobarb and vodka didn't mix, or maybe it was epilepsy and vodka. Certainly, during his illness, Matt didn't drink at all — not that he ever did much drinking. So when he joined Famous

People Players and went off to New York to open at Radio City Music Hall, I gave instructions in the letter requested of each parent that Matthew not be allowed to drink any kind of alcoholic beverage — beer, wine, anything.

Does everyone know about Famous People Players? They are a black-light puppet theatre created and directed by a forceful woman named Diane Dupuy. She keeps it an open secret that of the fifteen-or-so members of her company, thirteen are mentally handicapped, from mildly to severely. (Numbers may vary.) Through a series of circumstances, Matthew joined her company, filling in for a performer who had broken her ankle and who was unable to rejoin them in time for the next tour. Matthew missed his sister's wedding because his opening in New York was the same day.

I flew down to see him (and check on him) immediately after the wedding, taking in the show and seeing the arrangements made for the company. Does everyone know about show biz? Eating hours and bedtimes are late and odd, and food often merely expedient or convenient without being particularly nutritious. I have since discovered in a fact sheet about nutrition and epilepsy that one recommendation outweighs all others: "Do not make drastic changes in your eating habits without consulting your physician!" (The exclamation mark is mine.) In other words, as in many other cases, a well-balanced nutritious diet is a must, particularly when a chronic disorder exists. Too much or too little of certain chemicals may cause the seizure threshold to be lowered. This is why some doctors have pursued the junk-food path, attempting to eliminate oversalted, overspiced, and overprocessed foods from the diets of hyperactive children, for example. Such a caution could well be applied to epileptics.

Every night after the show at Radio City Music Hall, Matt and the other members of the company would pig out on chips and pizza, pop and chocolate bars, before they went to bed. They would sleep in, eat brunch before the afternoon show, and an early dinner (between 4 and 5 P.M.) before the evening show. After that, they threw themselves on the mercies of room service, at their own expense and indiscretion. Matthew was having a ball — and forgetting to take his Dilantin.

I went home the following weekend. On the Monday, their first day off since they opened, the kids all went to see the Statue of

Liberty and to Mama Leone's for a bang-up Italian dinner, at which Matt drank who knows how much red wine. The next morning, in the twilight zone between sleeping and waking, Matthew had a seizure. Dupuy called an ambulance and shot him off to the hospital where he was released immediately. But she found out that the ambulance driver was a friend or relative of someone who worked at Radio City Music Hall, and she was worried that if this story got back there, no one would trust the company. Therefore, she fired Matthew. She told me she was sending him home on the next plane.

"You can't tell me," I said, "that with a company of handicapped people, you don't have another epileptic in the group."

"Oh, yes," she said, "but no one ever had a fit on me before. I can't take the risk."

Epileptics still inspire a primitive fear in people, even those who are dedicated to helping the mentally handicapped. Imagine what discrimination is practised by those who are less knowledgeable!

> Discrimination in the workplace and at school is a serious problem even for those 60 per cent who are well controlled by drugs.
>
> Adults with epilepsy have indicated that finding employment is their greatest problem. Twenty five per cent of employable people with epilepsy are unemployed – over three times the national average. Studies in the United States over the past thirty years show that the disability that poses the greatest barrier to employment is epilepsy.
>
> Public education is one of the greatest needs, as most people know so little about epilepsy. Negative public attitudes create a greater disability than the medical condition itself. (from a fact sheet published by the Epilepsy Association of Metro Toronto)

I took Matt back to the psychiatrist he was seeing at the time to make sure the disappointment and shame of being fired were not too much for him to handle. Matt was very philosophical about it.

"I have this problem," he told the doctor, "and it's okay. But Diane hit the panic button. It's really *her* problem."

There are two types of seizure, generalized or partial. *Gener-*

alized seizures include what we call convulsions, *tonic-clonic*, which can be quite frightening to an onlooker, and a *simple absence* seizure. In the olden days, these two generalized types used to be called "grand mal" and "petit mal," indicating the kind of drama surrounding epilepsy. In a *grand mal*, or *tonic-clonic*, the sufferer may fall to the floor, eyes rolled back, muscles stiffened. He may breathe heavily, and his body may jerk rhythmically. Sometimes the tongue falls back into the throat and must be pulled out to prevent suffocation; sometimes the tongue gets bitten and the person's mouth may be bloody. Saliva is usually hard to control and the person drools, or "foams at the mouth." The convulsion may last from two to five minutes, and seldom hurts the person beyond a residual headache. Grand mal affects all ages. Hospitalization is seldom necessary.

The *simple absence* seizure, or *petit mal*, occurs mainly in children. The child seems to be having a staring spell or be daydreaming for five to fifteen seconds. Perhaps the face will twitch slightly, involuntarily, or the eyes may roll up or to one side. The child will probably not know what has happened. If someone doesn't recognize these symptoms and find the cause and treat them, the result can be a serious learning problem. It's the circuitry of the brain that's involved. If a circuit breaks, it must be attended to.

Then there are partial seizures: *complex partial* (psychomotor or temporal lobe) and *simple partial* (focal). Only a portion of the brain is affected. Strange sensations, fears, and distortions of the environment probably frighten the sufferer more than his observers. He may pluck at his clothes or books, smack his lips, wander around aimlessly (so that explains why Matt sometimes picked holes in his pants or socks). The person may not lose complete consciousness but may be unable to remember anything that happened during the seizure, and be confused for a while afterwards. Matt scared us a couple of times when he wandered off and was unable to account for several hours in his day, turning up too late at an appointment or a program and too confused to be able to tell anyone where he had been. Fortunately, that hasn't happened very often.

What do you do when a person has a seizure? The same thing

my mother used to tell me people do when it rains in China. You let it rain. Don't restrain him but do protect him from dangers like falling against something sharp or suffocating on his own tongue. If the seizure is a general one, loosen his clothing, check that tongue, and try to roll him to one side for easier breathing and to prevent the tongue from falling back into his throat again. Don't give him something to bite, or try to force anything into his mouth. If it's a partial, talk reassuringly. He won't remember anything you've said later, but the sound of your voice will be comforting. That's when Matt talks about his father, calling for him and asking him why he left. I find Matt's poignant words very painful, but he doesn't remember them.

I remember when I was in grade school a boy named Pooh (his real name was Hugh) used to stiffen and fall down straight as a board, always during assemblies. I never understood what happened to him or what caused these spasms, but I can remember thinking he had a rare talent. What a neat way to get out of a boring assembly! The other kids used to say, usually in a sing-song rhythm, "Poohie has fits, Poohie has fits." Somehow, I don't think kids have changed much since then.

Did you know that over 6 per cent of the population has at least one seizure during their lifetime? One per cent of the population suffers from one of the types of epilepsy. In Canada, that's about 200,000 people — more than the number that suffers from cancer, tuberculosis, multiple sclerosis, and cerebral palsy put together.

So Matthew is "slightly" epileptic. He has been lucky (still counting) that his seizures — the grand mal kind — have occurred when he was at home in bed. The last one, about a year and a half ago as I write this, happened, we think, because he had 'flu and was running a fairly high temperature. (You've heard about overheated brains? It's true!) The one before that was about two years earlier. Still, there is always the possibility of an inconvenient or dangerous occurrence, so Matt wears a Medic Alert bracelet identifying his problem, so that strangers or policemen will not think he is drunk and disorderly if he suddenly falls down in the street.

We have both learned to live with uncertainty, but haven't let it govern us. Probably because I have such grasshopper optimism, I never think that disaster will befall until it does. So I have never forbidden any activity out of fear that Matt will have a seizure. I am told this is a valuable attitude to have. Restricting a child's activity out of fear would be likely to damage his emotional growth.

According to another fact sheet about epilepsy, only the most extremely dangerous activities, such as diving and mountain climbing, are forbidden. Other potentially dangerous activities must be regulated according to the person's history of seizures, the length of warning he might have, and his ability to recognize his warning signals. For anyone who suffers from seizures, a buddy system is mandatory, not only for swimming and such, but for day-to-day living. Matthew could never be left alone overnight, for example, because of his twilight-zone history. He must never live alone (not a bad thing).

It is possible for an epileptic to obtain a driver's licence. Here is some information from the Driver Control Section, Ontario Ministry of Transportation and Communications:

> It is the responsibility of the patient's physician to report any conditions which he feels may impair a person's ability to drive or may endanger other drivers or pedestrians. This, of course, includes epilepsy, but does not mean that every case must be reported. If the physician feels that the seizures are properly controlled, he is under no obligation to make a report to the Ministry. This applies to both prospective drivers and licensed drivers.

If you're shocked that epileptics are allowed to drive, then start examining your own prejudices. Personally, I'd rather a driver have epilepsy, controlled by drugs, than have a drinking problem. Who controls that?

As for employment and the type of work that can be done, for example, the use of power tools, again the emphasis lies in monitoring, not in omitting, the activity. Between 1945 and 1957, according to my fact sheets, a Workers' Compensation Board study showed 8.1 out of 1,000 accidents resulted from epileptic seizures, whereas 20.2 out of 1,000 resulted from coughing or sneezing.

As with everything else connected with your special child, each case must be treated individually. A lot can now be achieved with judicious medication that enables an epileptic to live a normal life. The problem, as Matthew pointed out, is no longer his. It's the problem of the people around him.

CHAPTER TEN

PERSECUTION

Mothers throughout history have shown great ferocity when protecting their children. They have thrown themselves under the wheels of chariots, plunged into whirlpools, run through fire, and fought lions for the sake of a child. Mothers have been known to move mountains, and to lift two-ton trucks. But what can a mother do to prevent society from hurting her child's feelings, damaging his ego, making him feel inadequate, and denying him friendship? All one can do is to build the strength into the child. Because a parent can't fight a child's battles for him. No one can.

We had had some forewarning of teasing and rejection in Matt's life before I discovered the battered apple. The little girl who followed him home with taunts and the little boy who teased him were simply more persistent than most. There is a natural selection process that children practise in choosing their friends that is as ruthless as that of any restricted club. You can't fight that kind of discrimination, or deny that it exists. Matt was a friendly little boy and I was an encouraging sort of mother, so he usually had playmates. He had wonderful toys and in Stratford he had a swimming pool, and these were definite social assets. I invited kids for lunch and for the night, and besides his annual birthday party, Matt (and his siblings and his parents) had pool parties, sleigh-ride parties, Hallowe'en parties, fireworks parties, barbecues, and excursions. A rich, full life, you might say.

If the friends Matt played with were usually a little younger than he was chronologically, that was to be expected as the gap widened between his age and his education and abilities. The little boy who began by teasing him became his best friend and our two neighbouring families were very close. Another boy, bright and Matt's own age, seldom played with Matt on a one-to-one basis; nevertheless he enjoyed being with Matt in a neighbourhood group, especially around our pool. You can call this a form of bribery on my part, blatantly inviting kids to come and play with us and Matt in our backyard, and you're absolutely right, but it was pleasant for all concerned.

So I was unprepared for the battered apple, the mangled sandwich, and the broken lunchbox. In that order. First of all, the apple. Matt was by this time in a special-ed class at a senior public school in Stratford and was taking his lunch. I found the apple, all bruised and mashed, when I was unpacking his lunchbox to prepare it for the next day.

"What happened to your apple?" I asked.

"It dropped," said Matt.

"It looks more as if it's been thrown," I said.

"Yes," he said. "They were throwing things."

The next thing "they" threw was a sandwich. I lifted a mushy mess out of the lunchbox a few days later.

"What happened to your sandwich?" I asked.

"I couldn't eat it," Matt said.

"I can see that," I said. "What happened?"

"We were playing."

I let it go. But when he came home with a broken lunchbox, I really started asking questions. It seems there were some big kids, one or two boys, in grade eight, who were teasing and bullying Matt, first in the lunchroom, then on the playground. I spoke to the principal of the school about it, the same one who had known Matt in his first school in Stratford, and who had ordered his teachers there to look the other way when John protected his little brother. He couldn't do much about the playground incidents, but he saw to it that there was more teacher supervision in the lunchroom. I told Matt to play with a buddy and to avoid the playground — not too difficult since there was no recess in a secondary school.

There are always the catcalls in any playground, right from the beginning. The slow learners and the special-ed kids always get called retards and dummies and slowpokes. The brash, swaggering kids with problems of their own seem to need someone to look down on, and the awkward, slow and ingratiating dummies are easy prey. Is kindness an innate quality? Are some people really born without it? Can't it be taught? Or do parents ever bother to teach qualities like kindness, tolerance, patience, generosity, and compassion?

We knew a little girl who had a withered arm and a dragging foot from birth. She was bright and pretty and did very well, but she, too, suffered from derision and scorn because she couldn't jump rope and run around and keep up with her playground peers. One day a boy was teasing her and she turned on him.

"You can see my problem," she said. "Yours is worse – it's in your head!"

So maybe those kids had problems, but they became Matt's problem, too. You can't go and make all playgrounds safe for "dummies." So you have to find ways for the dummy to protect himself, non-violent ways, preferably.

I knew some of the techniques from my own experience. I wasn't slow at school; I was too bright. And I was fat. I used to be accused of reading the dictionary every night. I was accused of studying. I was called Bessie, Jumbo, Dumbo, and Fatso, and I still remember who called me those names after all these years, and they still hurt. Grown-ups, of course, hide their barbs. They find other, more subtle, witty ways to put down others. Sometimes I think out-in-the-open is best, because if you protest a hidden or jocular insult you are accused of having no sense of humour. "Just a joke" at any age still hurts, maybe even more so when it's subtle. There really is no defence, but one has to try.

So I told Matthew what my mother used to tell me. "Just ignore them," she'd say. "Walk away. Don't give them the satisfaction of knowing they bother you." That took a lot of courage and some acting ability. I used to square my shoulders and walk away from the catcalls behind my back, promising myself that some day they'd be sorry, some day I'd be famous, and then they'd be glad they knew me – all the comforting fantasies I could think of.

That didn't help Matthew much, though. That was then, this was now, and he wasn't fat, he was just right, and he wasn't smart, he was slow.

Mother also used to say, "Laugh with them. Accept the joke. Make fun of yourself before they can." I tried that, too, but it backfired. I supplied some of the funniest lines against me, and some of the best nicknames. I was much more inventive than my tormentors and I put my weapons into their hands. Not a great idea. I couldn't recommend that as a method to Matthew. Besides, it wasn't funny. No, the best solution for Matthew seemed to be avoidance. Stay out of the playground; be sure there is a buffer (a teacher) in the lunchroom; wait for the problem to go away. Sometimes problems do go away, not often, but sometimes. In this case, we went away. We moved to Toronto.

Jesse Ketchum is a real inner-city school, at the corner of Bay and Davenport, in Toronto. After I had a brief consultation with various powers-that-be, Matt was placed in that school in a special-ed class. As I remember it, life was fairly uneventful during Matt's first year there. We had a lot of other things to adjust to, and I don't remember any particular problems to do with persecution in the playground. But it assumed huge proportions very quickly in his second year, and it was because of it that we eventually made the decision to take Matt out of the public school system the following year.

I knew it as soon as I found a mangled sandwich in his lunchbox. It was happening again. I asked if there was a teacher on duty. Theoretically, yes, but he or she didn't stay in the lunchroom the whole time. Someone was in the school, that's all. The kids were given a brief time to eat, and then were encouraged to go outside. If there was no activity in the schoolground, or if it was too cold, there were all kinds of shops and underground shopping malls just three blocks away at Bay and Bloor.

When the mashed, uneaten lunches continued to be brought home, I spoke to Matt's special-ed teacher about it. Yes, she had noticed what was going on, and she had conducted discussions about it in class, recognizing the harsh laws of the schoolground and the unanswerable and implicit blackmail that went on. Blackmail, certainly. If a kid complained to the teacher about his treatment and named names, the culprits might be reprimanded, but there would be worse treatment waiting for the squealer the next time a teacher's back was turned, or when there was no teacher present at all. Better for a kid to take his lumps than to rat on his tormentors.

Matt's teacher recommended a buddy system. If her charges tried to stick together there might be some safety and protection in numbers, even in a pair of them. This, obviously, was not always possible. There were times, and it seemed lunchtime was one of them, when Matt was alone and without the support of his comrades-in-arms.

His teacher and I also discussed the need to instil some strength and aggressiveness in the child. Matt is an affable, gentle boy, and far too trusting. He's like Charlie Brown with his football; he gets sucked in and fooled every time. Every year Lucy offers a football for Charlie Brown to kick, and every year she uses a different ploy and fools him into hurting himself. So with Matthew. He never stops trusting people. And he is quite passive, generally. He seldom gets angry, or if he does, he seldom shows his anger — a fault, really, that I didn't realize was hurting him. He puts up with too much for his own good, without complaining. How, then, do you teach a child like that to stand up for his rights? Without skill or strength or cunning or buddies, perhaps the best defence was retreat.

I am by nature a non-violent person, and Matt knows this better than anyone. "You're not going to like this," he'd say, as he said when he came home from his first scout meeting in Toronto.

"But you're going to tell me," I'd say, and he would. At that scout meeting, for example, a boy had been riding Matt unmercifully and my gentle, pacifist son had finally picked up the nearest object to stop the kid with. The nearest object happened to be a chair. Fortunately it was fairly heavy, so Matt couldn't swing it at his tormentor and make contact before the scoutmaster intervened.

I was really upset when Matt told me, much more than the scoutmaster was when I talked to him about the incident. He thought Matt was justified in his anger, although he admitted the kid should find more acceptable ways of demonstrating it. That was before I had realized how much I had suppressed Matt's expressions of anger over the years. The scoutmaster spoke to the other boy's parents, too, to try to work something out. In the end, the other boy left the scout troop. He had more problems than Matt, or different ones.

So when all else failed, we (the teacher and I) recommended that Matt take his lunch down to one of the underground shopping malls, buy a drink, and eat there. Shortly before Christmas, when

I was racing around that particular mall at lunchtime, picking up some extra goodies for stocking presents, who should I see racing along the walkway with a face like thunder and looking as if demons were after him but my son Matt?

"Whoa," I said. "Slow down. What's the matter?"

It seems his tormentors had caught on to his retreat tactics and this day they had followed him down Bay Street with their catcalls and taunts, all the way to the shopping mall. It was like the protection racket; there seemed to be no defence. I took Matt for lunch and walked him back to the school for another chat with the teacher. The Christmas holidays were almost upon us. We left the matter in abeyance until the New Year.

I'm not sure what happened then. The problem was not solved, but it mended slightly. Teachers were alerted; the buddy system was put into force; Matt suffered with grace. And I have already described to you his act of good humour and defiance on his graduation day from that school. I wonder if anyone learned anything from that. Besides Matt and me, I mean.

There really doesn't seem to be any defence against such mindless cruelty. When Matt was in the hospital in London I read him a book called *Hey, Dummy* by Kin Platt. It's about a severely retarded boy and a boy who befriends him and makes all sorts of painful discoveries about himself, his friends, his parents, and society. It's a harsh book; it doesn't pull any punches. Matt has never forgotten it and still refers to it. Of course, he is not nearly as retarded as the boy in the story, but he identified closely with him, having suffered some of the same callously cruel treatment at the hands of his schoolmates.

One of the most painful things parents have to bear when they have a handicapped child is the unfeeling discrimination and the cruel persecution with which the child is frequently treated, not only by his peers but by other, and presumably mature, members of society. All of us perform incredible daily acts of discrimination and violence against people who are least able to protect themselves.

And yet there are rules, and one must obey them, or suffer the consequences. I mentioned the junior counselling job Matt had at a Y day camp. He was fired from it for hitting a kid. He still remembers it, and the frustration and the anger. I asked him recently how he felt about teasing. (He's still being teased, by the way.)

"I don't say much," he said. "I just leave them alone."

"But what do you do?" I persisted.

"I don't use my anger that much," he said. "Sometimes I swear... sometimes at people. I get huffy and I want to punch people but I shouldn't because I'll get in trouble. I did that once. I put my knee in a seven-year-old's stomach—by accident. I didn't mean it. The kid teased a lot. I'd had enough. Leave me alone, I said. It wasn't nice of me to do that."

So now he lets it go. It's the only safe way to behave.

People have their own reasons for hating, fearing, and persecuting those who are different. Not the least of them are assumptions we make about others, unfounded or not. People who suffer from cerebral palsy are mistakenly considered to be drunk or insane by strangers who see them shuffling down the street, lurching on or off buses, or trying to communicate with their slow, slurred speech. People who look stupid or who respond slowly (making change, answering questions) are also treated differently. (We make other decisions about people and behaviour: young people are careless; beautiful people are good—but sometimes selfish; handsome men are competent—but spoiled; tall people are strong and reliable; short people aren't as competent—and so they become aggressive—and so on.)

In a way, the process is a vicious circle: we impose the face on the behaviour and assume the behaviour from the face. In a book intended for actors, *Impro*, by Keith Johnstone, about improvisation in the theatre, the author devotes a chapter to masks. A mask, he says, "is a device for driving the personality out of the body and allowing a spirit to take possession of it." The faces we assume become like masks. Who decides on the faces we will carry? Somewhere along the way we made a decision, or a decision was made for us. Johnstone says, "Even in very young people you can see that a decision has been taken to appear tough, or stupid, or defiant. (Why should anyone wish to look stupid? Because then your teachers expect less of you.)"

Johnstone goes on to comment on the "deadness" of expression that most adults cultivate as their public face. (Look at anyone in a bus or subway train, in an airport or a train station, if you don't believe him.) Grown-ups have learned to mask their fears and their sense of incompetence (and wonder). Johnstone attributes the following idea to John Holt (*How Children Fail*), but the words are his:

> A fourteen-year-old with a mental age of six doesn't "act six" because we won't let him, but he can't "act fourteen" either, so he looks stupid as a defense. A child of one and a half can look bright and alert, but an adult with a mental age of ten has to look like a moron because this is the most acceptable persona he's able to assemble. When retarded children [are allowed] to behave spontaneously, we see at once that deadness was only a cloak, a crippling disguise.

I guess we're all victims of our self-images. I still have a "fat" psyche left over from when I was a child. Matthew has a perception of himself, reinforced by society, as a loser, a meek one, but a valuable, lovable personality for all that. For years, we — my family and I — imposed that lovable image on him. He was our sunshine, our bright one, our happy, golden boy. As it turned out, this imposition was not in his best interests, either.

CHAPTER ELEVEN

BREAKDOWN

Just when you think you're in the clear, that's when you have to watch out, that's when your troubles begin. Matthew was in good shape the fall of 1978. After bouncing in and out of a haphazard educational system, and not learning very much, suffering discrimination and persecution, surviving the death of his father, moving to a strange city, losing his neighbourhood friends, adjusting to a new school, and finally, it seemed, overcoming his epilepsy, Matthew had the brightest future ahead of him for the coming year that he had ever faced. On the advice of a neurological pediatrician I had cut him off the phenobarbital he had been taking as an anticonvulsant. He was functioning more clearly and was looking forward to his work in his tough boarding school, where he was actually beginning to learn something.

At the end of September he had another seizure. That was the chief catalyst, but there other contributing factors to the downward spiral of anxiety he fell into. I'll try to analyze them, because it might help other parents when they consider the pressures their special children face as they emerge from their childhood into the more demanding teen years and become fearful of the future.

Matthew was seventeen years old that fall. A boy he travelled to and from school with on weekends had already passed eighteen. His friend kept telling him that eighteen was very tough, that rather than signalling the beginning of adulthood, a good thing, it meant the end of childhood and irresponsibility. "You really have to deliver now," the boy warned Matt, "or else they'll turf you out."

Shape up or ship out—a familiar phrase to us, but threatening to these kids who weren't ready to be on their own. The thought scared Matt.

He was very aware of his release from the phenobarb. He was earning some legitimate praise for the work he was doing and for his increased clarity. When he had the seizure and was immediately put back on the drug, he felt that it was a backward step, a loss for him. The paper bag was descending over his head again, and he started fighting his way out of it, becoming very hyper and nervous and tense, trying too hard, worrying too much.

Then on the day of his seizure he came home to find his easily achieving brother there, celebrating his birthday, and probably felt some pangs of jealousy. If Matt were not as smart or sensitive, he wouldn't be so aware of his position in relation to society or to his siblings. But he's smart enough to know what he's missing, and that hurts. I know some more severely retarded children whose inability hurts their parents far more than it hurts them, because they don't know any better. They don't know enough to compare themselves to others. Their achievements are within their own context. Within their limited range they function quite happily and well. Most learning-disabled children are not granted that peace. There is a constant gap between their desire and their actual achievement, between the goals they and society set, and their fulfilment of those goals. Brighter ones than Matthew, fiercely frustrated by their simple dyslexia (*nothing* is simple), often become morose and belligerent in their teens because of this painful gap.

And so with Matthew. Try as he would, it seemed there was no way out of his paper bag or the trap of his life. He had hit a Catch-22: no matter how hard he tried he couldn't make it. Everything seemed designed to thwart him.

The school principal left and was replaced by a new one. Matt missed the old one and somehow took his departure as a personal blow. He came home for a couple of weekends after the crucial time. On each successive visit he seemed more anxious, but more spaced-out as well. Finally, by Thanksgiving, the school deemed that he was unable to come home.

Liz was studying in Montreal that year; Kate was travelling in Europe. John and I had dinner with friends on Sunday and he went back to Guelph to study. Thanksgiving Monday I drove over to see Matt and took him out to a fried-chicken place for our Thanksgiving dinner together. He was in bad shape—tense, frightened, and drugged, on prescription by the school physician.

I guess it was about a month after that when the school director phoned me and said they couldn't do anything more for Matt, that he had to go into a hospital for treatment, that it was likely a "long-term psychosis" and it would take a long time for him to get better, if he ever did. I made arrangements for Matthew to be admitted to the Clarke Institute of Psychiatry in Toronto, and met a couple of the teachers who brought Matt in. I had been travelling and Matt hadn't been home, so I hadn't seen him for a couple of weeks. I was shocked at the slack-jawed, shuffling, glazed-eyed wreck of a boy I saw.

Mental illness assaults the minds and the hearts of the people who love its victim. It is painful to see your child looking like that, so lost and uncontrolled, like a derelict or a wino unaccepted by society.

It's pride, too. "He's not like that," you want to shout at people. "That's not the real Matthew. You don't know him. You don't know what he's really like."

Matt managed to stay soap-and-water clean in the hospital, but the side effects of the drugs created some unattractive problems. He salivated a lot and was barely aware of it, so he drooled. I used to drape a towel around his neck so he could wipe his mouth and chin. He looked like a superannuated tennis pro. He shook too, with a tremor that eventually made him lose a lot of weight. Between the drool and the tremor he didn't eat much, so that contributed to his weight loss, too. He looked like a starving refugee after a few weeks, and fitted into clothes he had outgrown the previous year. His physical condition made my heart ache for him.

It also hurts to guess at the anguish within, the inescapable snake pit of emotions and fears that has trapped one's child. In spite of all the drugs thrust upon him like some sort of chemical straitjacket, Matthew was clearly suffering. He couldn't express much of it then, and he doesn't remember much of it now—a blessing.

"I felt rotten," he says, trying to recall the essence of what turned out to be a three-month stay. "I was like a boxer without a rematch, with my white towel around me."

"'Wipe your mouth,' people would say.

"The drugs were like a balloon — too much air."

We met a young woman in the ward the very first day. She came up to me and held out her hand. She had three pennies in her palm. "I have three cents," she said. "Will you take one? It's a chip on my shoulder." I hesitated. "Take one," she urged. "Then I'll have my two cents' worth," and she thrust out her hand for me to take a penny. I saw that her hands were shaking. It wasn't only the drugs.

"Are you scared?" I asked.

"Yes," she said.

"Would you like a hug?" I asked.

"Yes," she said.

So I opened my arms and I hugged her.

Everyone needs hugs. I hugged Matt a lot during that ordeal. I think hugs were the only thing that kept us both going.

"They told me I was going on a holiday," Matt said that first evening, after he had been admitted and settled in his ward. "This isn't a holiday. This is a hospital."

"Yes," I said. "Remember I went to hospital when my ulcers blew. I'm better now. You're in hospital because your head blew, and you're going to be better." I hoped he would be better. No one was making any predictions at this stage. I held his poor, dear, tight, racked, frightened body in my arms and tried to comfort him.

You think you know what pain and loneliness are, and then you learn some more. Matthew got worse before he got better. A whole lot worse.

Others have suffered through this, too, and they too have sought sources of comfort — not only for strength for themselves but also for extra reserves to give their suffering one. The best advice I can give is this: "Make yourself a channel for the divine energy to flow through and focus on him."

It's a kind of faith-healing. Every day you pray for strength, and you meditate and you build your reserves. And then every day you go to the hospital and you spend all that strength. I was strong and full of love for Matt each day, and then on the way out of the building I would deflate, so drained and helpless and full of pain myself that I wondered how I would get through the next day.

But every day I would go again and hug Matt and smile and play cards and chat and never ask about the future.

There are definite stages in the course of a mental illness. First, there is the fear and the confusion, not really helped — but I suppose alleviated — by the drugs. Next there is the anger. And then there is the depression. Then there is fear again. Always there is the pain, brought on by so many things: being locked up, for one. After a while, though, the prison begins to seem like a haven, and it is the "outside" that holds terror. Outside is where it happened, where you couldn't cope, where you'd have to go again and perhaps fail again. Pain is also imposed by one's own personal demons, whatever it is that's eating holes in one's faith and confidence. Other patients cause pain, too. Even in the hospital where other people were fellow-sufferers, Matt couldn't escape persecution.

Many people who suffer mental illness are bright, with normal I.Q.s, or at least with functioning, straightforward intelligence, unhindered by short circuits in the brain. I thought at the time that Matt was rare in suffering his illness, a condition brought about in part by his perception of the gap between his handicap and his expectations. In the course of my investigations later, it seemed to me that in fact a large number, perhaps a disproportionate number, of l.d. people suffered from mental illness, perhaps caused by their failures and their disappointments and pressures. But when I tried to pursue this idea with experts, they wouldn't agree. No statistics have been compiled on the incidence of mental illness among brain-injured people, but apparently it is no higher than the percentage of illness among normal people. It all depends on how a person handles the stress in his life, I was told. I'm not so sure. At least, let's acknowledge the amount of stress handicapped people experience.

Whatever the percentages, Matthew was the only l.d. person in his ward, and many people didn't know what his bottom line was, that is, his normal bottom line, when he wasn't sick as well. (The psychiatrist didn't know, either, but we'll get to that.) So there were patients who were impatient with him, who couldn't follow his conversation or understand his speech, who were repelled by his drooling, who wanted him to play cards with them and talk to them and who gave up in disgust when he couldn't or wouldn't cooperate. Giving up was one thing; overt cruelty and anger and persecution were not acceptable ways to deal with him. But I think it was his illness more than his handicap that prompted the doctor finally to assign one staff member to Matthew as daily monitor, to watch over him and also to protect him from attack.

And then Matthew's own lovable qualities asserted themselves in spite of the force field of drugs surrounding them, and some patients became his guardians and defended him against the angry ones. I know, not only because they talked to me and told me about it, but because I witnessed some of their protection. They protected me, too. There's a lot of kindness in the world, and some of the people who practise it best are those who need it most themselves.

The psychiatrist decided early on that Matt's was a case of incomplete bereavement. I disagreed. He asked for my book about widowhood to examine it for evidence of his theory, and had the ward staff read it, too. It was the first time my book had been used for that purpose, and I commented on that to some fellow members-of-the-board of Community Contacts for the Widowed, on which I sat. Two of them who worked at the Clarke expressed rueful despair over the doctor's request. They had recommended my book several times for use by all staff members, but this was the first time anyone had finally used it—but for such a different purpose! Not knowing Matt's bottom line, knowing very little about brain-injured people, I gathered, the psychiatrist clung to his theory. (Later, he called in another doctor more specialized in dealing with the mentally handicapped.) But other people on the ward—other patients—understood that Matt had dealt with his grief in a positive way.

"Your son has helped me," said one young woman in her midtwenties. Another young woman and her widowed mother also spent a lot of time talking to Matt, and getting help from him, they told me. All those games of homonyms, you see, had done their work. Certainly the pain never goes away, but one does develop scar tissue, and there is comfort in sharing one's sorrow and talking about it. And so Matt was able to help other people. Grief was not his problem.

Anger was. It took a while for me to learn how much we had deprived Matt of his legitimate expression of anger for the bad deal life had given him. He had always been our sunshine boy, so bright and pleasant, so even-tempered. He was "sunny." Actually, his father was, too. Bill's sister used that word of him on the day of his funeral. "He was always sunny," she said, and he was. He didn't visit his anger or frustrations on people. If things ever got beyond his control, which was seldom, he would take a walk or go to his room. I think he prayed.

Anyway, in temperament, Matt was most like his father. He had his father's sunny outlook and his humour. But one tends to lean on someone like that and to expect that kind of sunshine never to be clouded over. When I look back on it now, I wonder how Matt managed to maintain his even exterior and his wonderful equanimity for so long. How frustrated he must have been over the years, when his fingers and tongue wouldn't respond to the signals of his brain. How discouraged he must have felt when his body wouldn't perform the way he saw other people's bodies performing. How much loneliness and pain he must have suffered when he was cast off by yet another so-called friend, or teased by someone else who had seemed to be a comrade. But I – we – never let him express those feelings.

Matt split me, not himself, into two different people. I came to the hospital one day and he looked at me and said, "Well, it's Bitch B.J." B.J., of course, is my nickname, but Matt had never called me anything but Mom in his life. Now I was "B.J. the Bitch." He had to call me that to keep me separate in his mind from his mother, whom he needed and loved. But all those years of my bossing him around, of my impatience, of my unreasonable demands, of my fussing and worrying – in short, of my mothering – all those years during which he had never complained, never rebelled, never turned and expressed his rage, had to be dealt with, had to be released. His nurse used to take him down to the gym and encourage him to kick shit (sorry, but there is no other way to say it) out of a volleyball. Or she would tell him to go into his room and shut the door and pound his pillow and scream. And scream and scream. But it was his own idea to split me and rip me apart.

I didn't flinch. Each day I kept praying for that strength to flow through me when I was with my son, and it did, at least for the time I was with him. One night he said something really hurtful. I can't remember what it was now; selective forgetfulness has wiped it from my mind. At the time, though, I did not change expression or appear to react. I know, because I was aware of the control it took not to react. But Matt must have heard my internal scream, because he took his bitch-mother's hand in his and kissed it, another gesture he had never made. I think my heart cracked that day.

I was staggering then as I had never done, not even when my husband died. At such times of concern with one's child, the anxiety can only be shared by the other parent. I shut myself off from people and focused on Matthew. Not that other people were that eager to thrust their attentions upon me. There is still a stigma attached to mental illness that renders people helpless. They're terrified of it and they don't know what to do. It has been said, and I've said it myself, that when you lose a mate, you find out who your friends are. Well, when you have mental illness in the family, you find out even more. I started to joke that if I kept on finding out who my friends were I wouldn't have any left, but it was no joke. I still count among my dearest friends the few who remained loyal and helpful during that hard time, and who seemed to know, when I didn't, what I needed.

God knows I needed a lot. I was beginning to be unable to pray. I would kneel in anguish and all I could say was "Please, please, please." Always before I had been able to praise God and give thanks for my blessings. But now I had reached a paralysis I had never experienced. I wrote my cousin to tell her my problem. She wrote me back to reassure me.

"God hears," she said. "Your helpless cry is a prayer, and God hears." I struggled on. There was worse to come.

But the time has come for you to ask, as I asked myself, how much can you give to another human being before you begin to damage yourself, and him? There comes a time when you must begin to distance yourself, not only from the pain but from such close involvement. This is not to say that you should withdraw all support, but that you have to rethink your commitment. I have seen couples, mothers especially, who ruin their marriages and their lives in their misplaced devotion to a handicapped child. They keep him with them far too long, past their own ability to care for him, and past the point at which he would be able to begin a life of his own. And they do it in the name of love and selfless care, thinking that in sacrificing their lives they are saving his. Not so.

Tough love is the name given to the treatment of delinquent juveniles by parents who have been too lenient. The idea is that if support ceases the kid may eventually get the idea he has to straighten out, take care of himself, and stop looking to his parents to bail him out. The name should be applied to a treatment not usually given to handicapped and mentally ill people. There comes a time when some sort of withdrawal must take place, not only to guarantee the survival of the sufferer, but also to preserve the health and sanity of the care-givers. I am not in any way recommending total withdrawal, but I am saying that a judicious backing-off can be very helpful for all concerned. So I discovered when I had to start distancing myself from Matthew. At first it was simply an attempt at mental rehabilitation for myself. Never has it become abandonment. You can't do that. You can't abandon someone who needs you desperately, no matter how hard it is on you.

I looked up that line of St. Paul's during that time, and I found it helped:

> For God will not try you beyond what you are able, but together with the trial will give you the strength to endure it, and so provide you with a way out. — I Corinthians 10:13

The one thing I never could get over was the huge gap between what God thought I was able to endure and what I thought I could handle. Amazing! Well, one goes on.

Through all this, the psychiatrist assured me we were making progress. It was progress I couldn't see. Matt had progressed from fear and confusion to anger, to depression, and back to fear and confusion again. A couple of teachers came from his school and suggested that they bring him some work to do. He turned on them and yelled, "Don't push me!" Later, he explained to me, "I'm confused and frightened and lonely." I was, too. I was on the edge of tears all the time. I realized how much I had depended on Matt's strength and good cheer, on his patience and goodwill, on his tolerance, fortitude, and gentleness. I began to wonder who had been helping whom.

The psychiatrist thought I was a woman of steel, making too

many decisions, not leaning on him enough. Why, he asked me, did I behave like that, waiting patiently for his meetings, not yelping at the nurses, just coming quietly every day and talking to Matt and the other patients who were his friends?

When I did comment on the seeming lack of progress to the psychiatrist, he pointed out that Matt was no longer having any psychotic incidents. He was not hallucinating any more: voices no longer spoke to him from the television set; he no longer claimed to be meeting his geographically distant sisters or brother on the street or in the ward, as he had been claiming a few months earlier. That was progress. He had an attention span of about five seconds; he couldn't find his way out of a paper bag without help, let alone cross the street unattended. But it seemed he was getting better.

I think the profession has to do a great big public-relations job on the lay public if they're going to convince us of the value of the magical psychotropic drugs they use. I referred once with some distaste to the chemical straitjacket Matt was in, and the psychiatrist haughtily questioned my use of such a term, but without defending the drugs. He took them for granted; the lay public does not. Neither do mental patients. I know, I know, there's a use for them. They make the world a safer place, both for so-called normal people and for people who are mentally ill (and I think the line between them is closer than we think. Often, it seems to me, it rests on a label or on the sufferer's lack of discretion). But indiscriminate use of the drugs without adequate rehabilitation, support, therapy, and a concerted effort to reduce and eliminate them as soon as possible seems to me to be using them merely as a crutch, masking symptoms without seeking a cure for the cause. I was to learn a little more about this. At the time I was too naïve and too frightened of them.

Maybe it was because I was a doctor's daughter, and had learned better than to bother a doctor. I expected the psychiatrist to tell me all the answers in his own good time. (The time never came.) The psychiatrist, on his part, couldn't understand my attitude. He was used to women becoming hysterical or at least weepy and begging him to tell them what to do. Or so a friend who worked at the Clarke told me. She said psychiatrists are used to playing God in their patients' lives and can't understand, indeed, rather resent, anyone who tries to cope without breaking—particularly a woman.

I bring this up because I think that people do tend to be rather cowed by professionals, be they teachers or psychologists or psychiatrists or whatever. Parents of special children have to deal with professionals all their children's lives and become far too dependent on other people's decisions for their children's future. But you have to trust your own instincts as well. No one knows your child better than you do. By all means, accept professional guidance and be grateful for it, but don't let the experts put you down, or force you into decisions that are wrong for your child.

Obviously, Matt's psychiatrist and I did not see eye to eye, but Matt and I both had a wonderful relationship with his occupational therapist. She was another of Matt's conquests, and came to dinner at our home after Matt was discharged from hospital. It was not a professional call; she was his friend. She listened to Matt and talked to him on the outings he was beginning to take and the therapy he was enjoying (like cooking) with her. She told me something he said that I have remembered ever since.

Matt was talking about his eventual recovery and re-entry into the outside world. "What I have to do," he told her, "is jump back into the future."

I suppose that's the only way to look at it when the future is so frightening.

CHAPTER TWELVE

LIFE GOES ON

Matthew was going to be eighteen years old on February 7, 1979. He was still in the Clarke Institute and, as far as I could see, was worse off than when he entered. He was on a very heavy dosage of drugs, and even the drug prescribed to reduce the side effects didn't seem to have much effect. He had lost so much weight he looked like a walking hanger; his clothes hung on his emaciated body and he shook as if he had Parkinson's disease. He salivated and drooled and shuffled through each day, eyes glazed, with no apparent continuity in his thinking patterns, though he still suffered occasional lapses into fear, anguish, pain, and confusion.

In anticipation of Matt's birthday, I had ordered a big cake appropriately decorated with roses and greetings, for Matt to share at dinner with his fellow patients. I had arranged for a day pass for him, to take him shopping that morning and out for lunch. He was getting better on his passes. Earlier outings had sometimes been disastrous, particularly the Christmas one.

Our poor, glazed, drooling boy had sat at the Christmas dinner table shouting, "I want to go home."

"You are home," I said, but he couldn't tell. We had our plum pudding dessert one year later (well-ripened). His birthday pass would be well controlled, and happier than that, I was sure.

The day before Matt's birthday I had a meeting with a school representative, the psychiatrist, and a social worker to discuss Matt's eventual discharge. I was amazed to discover that the school representative expected to take Matt back to school *that day*! The reason for this haste was that if the school didn't have Matt back under its roof before his eighteenth birthday, he would not qualify for the government grants the school received on his behalf, and it needed the money.

The psychiatrist was not pleased at this turn of events; he liked to make these decisions. I was surprised, but practical.

"I'll cancel his birthday cake," I said. And when they were discussing weekends at home and the problem of Matt's getting there, since he couldn't use public transportation by himself in his current drugged condition, I agreed to meet him in Hamilton, saying, "The car knows the way." What else could I do but bow gracefully to circumstances? Bow? I was genuflecting at that point! By then, I was rolling with the punches, simply reacting to the immediate necessity of the moment. Thinking would come later. Right now we had to pack up Matt's few things from the hospital and arrange for him to leave the hospital that afternoon. The school representative helped me, and we had lunch before she took Matt away.

Events often seem to develop an impetus of their own and we have no control over them, seeking merely to catch up, to skate on one side, to be within coping distance. Experts make up their minds for us and for our children and tell us what's going to happen next and it seems all we can do is submit meekly. Certainly we need expert advice, certainly we have to follow guidelines, obey rules, bow to circumstance, but we also have to know our own child. The experts are not always right.

If you suspect you are being handed a judgement that sounds more like an accusation or an indictment of your loved one, then seek another opinion. Psychiatrists and all the other experts are not gods; they only act like it. They are human beings and they are fallible, as you and I are. Your child needs all the help he can get, and he may not always be helped by the arbitrary decisions that an "expert" makes. You have to stand fast and believe in yourself, and your child, as I did with Matthew.

I had to cling to that inner knowledge in the next few months. Most of my friends were shocked at the sight of Matthew and his very obvious problems. Since few of them had seen him in the hospital, they were entirely unprepared for this shambling, incoherent waif who demanded their attention in my living room. Matt's Big Brother, bless him, staying past the sixteen-year-old cut-off time with him, was so shocked at his appearance and behaviour at Christmas that he had trouble recovering. One older woman came to help me after Matt was home, taking me on errands and staying with Matt in her car while I ran in and out. But she used the time to tell me in no uncertain terms that I should lock Matt up permanently—and throw away the key.

As for his school, it couldn't cope. I finally had a long talk with the director, a young man whom I had been so grateful to for all he had done for Matthew. He told me, though, that he could do no more. Matt was ineducable as he was, drugged out of his skull. He was also vulnerable, more than ever, to the attacks of his harsh schoolmates; and he was at high risk. In short, I must take Matt home and keep him. The director had no further suggestions and very little hope to offer. Maybe an institution was best for the boy.

So Matt came home. The principal (not the director) of the school had done some sleuthing and found an organization that might be able to help Matt, if they were willing to take him on. Toronto Youth Services was funded by the Ministry for Community and Social Development (ComSoc) in the province of Ontario. Their mandate was to try to save disturbed adolescents, recover them while there was still time and hope for them. Matthew qualified as one for whom there was both. It took a few interviews and, I'm sure, several meetings on the part of the people involved, but help was on the way.

Here's how it worked: a teacher-nurse-companion-friend was found for the patient, and hired to work with him for twenty hours a week, helping him to re-enter the world, relearn the transit system and other life skills, find things to do, work out, whatever. The initial contract was for three months and was renewable upon review. It's called rehabilitation. It's also called a reprieve for the home front. That's when I discovered how many hours in a week there were (I had never thought about it before), because I was responsible for Matt the other 148 hours—his psychiatric nurse.

And so a very nice young man called Marty came into Matt's life. Fortunately, he had been in it before, having been a teacher at Matt's boarding school for a time, so he already knew my son. Unfortunately, he lived in St. Catharines, and I had to agree to pay his transportation in and out of Toronto for his meetings with Matt.

I took Matthew to my family doctor, Martin Taylor, the general practitioner who had known us since our move to Toronto (only four years by then, but he had a good idea of Matt's bottom line). Dr. Taylor was shocked at the change in Matt. Where was our bright, friendly, funny boy? Not here. Not in this frightened, confused, shuffling, drugged creature drooping in front of him. He knew very little about psychotropic drugs — they were hardly his field. Nevertheless, he got out his physician's pharmacy book and looked up Haldol and its side effects. He was as determined as I was to get Matt down, or up, as the case may be, off those drugs. In the beginning, it was like trying to fine-tune a radio with boxing gloves on, but we were both game to try it.

It was especially game of Dr. Taylor. The psychiatrist had sent what amounted to a threatening letter along with Matthew, warning anyone who tampered with the drugs and dosage he had prescribed that he would not be responsible for the results, and that any bad effects would be the fault of the doctor who dared to change or challenge his decisions. Our doctor took a drastic step, one that taught us both quite a lesson. He cut Matt off everything, all at once. Well, not the Dilantin, as I remember; Matt needed that to prevent the occurrence of a seizure. But everything else stopped.

Matt stopped sleeping. He would get up four and five times in the night and turn everything on: stove elements, television, radios, stereo, and lights. He would wander around the apartment taking books out of the shelves and piling them up anywhere. He would pull all his clothes out of his drawers and throw them around his room. He would pace and pace like a caged animal. And I would get up and try to talk him back into bed, giving him warm milk, rubbing his back, trying to make sense for my poor, demented son, and trying to believe that now we were making progress. He got away from me once, on a Sunday morning in early April, without a coat. I was ready to call the police to ask for help in finding him when he showed up with the calendar of an evangelical church in his hands, and strange stories I couldn't understand.

He couldn't be left alone for a minute. The hours he was with Marty were precious to me because, if they were well timed, I could try to get some work done. I had a radio show then and I had to come up with bright, optimistic copy for my daily diary. If I tried to work when Matt was at home, he would stand beside me and ask me when I was going to stop typing. We were discovering what life was like without drugs — or with increasingly less.

The doctor restored the dosage and then, over the weeks and months that followed, reduced them gradually. Our goal was no drugs at all (except for the Dilantin), but we had to take it slowly—we knew that now. Without them, Matt was too tense, too hyper. With them, he didn't think very clearly or respond very well.

I wasn't the only one who found that hard to live with. I found Marty one day stubbornly forcing Matt to cope with the two locks on my apartment door, expressing the same impatience and frustration that I was experiencing. One day they went jogging in a nearby park and Matt dirtied his pants. You tend to think that these basic errors are deliberate, that if he just made an effort, he could learn (relearn) the skills he had, control himself, respond, be competent, for heaven's sake! And so you become impatient, frustrated, maddened, discouraged, hysterical—yes, hysterical.

I finally broke one morning. I don't remember whether either of us had slept that night but morning came hard and early. I had to push Matt back into the shower because he came out still soaped all over. Every single thing he was doing was with less skill than when he was five years old, and with less enthusiasm. No enthusiasm at all, in fact. Just these drugged, mindless, horrible, slow-motion, underwater movements and this deadpan, unresponsive face and no expression whatsoever, no cries of pain or flashes of laughter. Nothing. You can understand why relatives of the mentally ill find them so difficult to live with. One becomes slightly mad oneself. I did. That morning, as Matt was fumbling with his shoelaces, unable (once more) to tie them, I started to scream.

"I can't stand it," I shouted at him. "I can't stand it any longer. Oh, Matthew, I hate you, I hate you!" And then I stopped—in horror at myself, at what I had said. I started to sob. And Matt looked at me with his calm, drug-glazed eyes and reassured me:

"You're just going through a phase, Mom," he said. And I laughed—hysterically.

Later that morning, at the bus depot, I said to Matthew, "We need a miracle, Matt. Do you think you could provide one?"

"Yes," he said, but he didn't know what I was saying. Or did he?

I put him on the bus for Hamilton with grave doubts. Little by little, Marty had been teaching Matt the transit system again, making appointments with him and trusting him to go a little farther and to find his way alone. But this was more than Matthew had attempted thus far. Matt was going to go for a visit to his boarding school for the weekend. Rather than drive all the way in from St. Catharines to Toronto and back again, Marty asked me to put Matt on the bus to Hamilton. He would meet the boy there and drive him to the school. But when Marty met the bus, Matt wasn't on it.

"Where's Matt?" Marty asked, when he phoned me. "Did you miss the bus?"

"No, I put him on it. I watched him until it pulled away," I said.

"He's not here," said Marty. "He wasn't on the bus. Maybe he got off at the other pick-up place in Toronto. You'd better call the police."

It's not easy to explain to a policeman about your missing son and his recent history in the Clarke and the high drug dosage he's on and the erratic behaviour he exhibits and just why he was on a bus alone in the first place. Marty kept phoning in to check with me. Having tried everything he could think of in Hamilton, he finally decided he would drive to Toronto. When he arrived, it was late afternoon and I asked if he had phoned the school. He hadn't.

"Don't you think you had better call and tell them what's happened?" I said.

Matt was at the school. He had delivered his miracle.

No one will ever be able to account fully for the three or four hours Matt spent wandering around Hamilton. As near as we could figure, he got off the bus at the first stop rather than waiting to get to the bus depot. Somewhere along the way he had lost his parka and his house keys, had picked up a library book someone had borrowed from the Hamilton Public Library (I mailed it back), and had finally walked into a Bell Canada office where he had asked to use the phone. He had the school number in his wallet, and he phoned and asked if someone could come and pick him up. All in all, I thought he had exhibited more rational behaviour than Marty and I had.

As far as I was concerned, that was Matt's turning point. I knew he would get better. I knew he would come back. I knew he could take care of himself. He would survive.

Not that it was easy after that, but there was steady progress. We were beginning to talk once more about his future. Marty's contract was renewed by ComSoc for another three months. We found some day programs for Matt to attend that summer, an afternoon one run by ComSoc, I think, and a morning one run by Famous People Players (that was when I made my first contact with that organization). What we had to find was a suitable school for the fall. More tests and assessments were in order.

What Matt found was the Haney Centre. Or rather, the Haney Centre was found for Matthew. I am still grateful that the Haney Centre took Matthew in. He was still recovering. He was by then on a low dosage of Haldol. He couldn't cope with much pressure. He needed companionship, activity, and some kind of non-threatening stimulation more than he needed to learn anything. Haney was his/my last resort, and it certainly was the best solution for that year.

Matthew was back at school, living at home. Life seemed to be resuming its normal proportions. We had other, private events that have little to do directly with this book. But one small incident was memorable. Matt actually lost his temper with his brother during that year and swore at him. John was shocked.

"Are you going to let him say that to me?" John asked me. "I didn't talk like that when I was his age."

"How old do you think he is?" I asked.

"He's—ohmigosh," John said. "He's nineteen!"

"Uh-huh. And what did you talk like when you were that age?" I asked.

That silenced John. The really important thing was that Matt had actually gotten angry. I now try to encourage him to do so when he has a legitimate beef. And when I'm unfair and get impatient with him, I stop and say, "Hey, wait a minute. I have no right to talk to you like that. Stop me. You don't have to put up with that." Sometimes he has stopped me without my telling him to. One time I was nagging him about something and he said to me, "You really can ride a person, can't you, Mom?" And I was so pleased! Also apologetic. It doesn't happen often enough. I still rant too much and he still puts up with too much from me.

Anyway, we were making progress. I have to keep telling myself that. At times, the progress seems to be merely another temporary solution, but I have to believe in it, give it my best shot, as they say. When I was doing the research for this book, I noticed the tone that frequently crept into a mother's voice when she answered a question about her child.

"How is your son getting along?" I would ask. "What's he doing this year?"

"Well," she would say, and that tone, that tired, fearful, anxious, quiet, resigned tone would colour her voice as she proceeded to tell me what "progress" he was making.

She knew. We all know. We just have to keep on trying.

CHAPTER THIRTEEN

GROUP HOMES AND ALTERNATIVES

Life presents different problems to a special adult. Now, if that isn't a simplistic statement! Just remember I'm talking about an adult with a built-in set of problems, the never-ending ones he was born with, whether it's brain damage or mental retardation or a minimal perceptual handicap. However well he may have learned to cope with them, they're still there. They don't go away. They must always be taken into account. Parents can usually handle his problems more easily when he is a child. Allowances are made because he is little, because perhaps he will "grow out of it," because there isn't too much difference between his care and handling and the treatment of a normal child. The gap widens, however, as he grows older, increasingly so. By the time he is a young adult, it is very clear that he is not "normal," usually in appearance as well as in behaviour.

Something happens to peoples' faces. Constant failure, frequent rejection, and nagging insecurity as well as lack of confidence begin to show in the eyes, in a kind of sunken look to the cheeks, in a set of the mouth, too placating or too belligerent. Somewhere along the way, in learning to get along in the world, these people develop a persona. (We all do.) Rarely does it fool anyone; it's a mask, and affords small protection. Maybe other kids no longer yell at them in the playground but there are still the sighs, the exaggerated patience, and the long-suffering faces of people they have to deal with daily as they try to cope with making change, giving orders (making requests), finding their way, and making their wants known. They don't look like cute little kids any more. They are full-grown, adult-sized people trying to get along in an indifferent, often cruel, world.

Their handicaps and disabilities vary, of course. Each person is a specific case. One's dyslexia (the problem with reading) may have rendered him functionally illiterate even though he is very bright. Another's more severe retardation may make his movements clumsy and his response time incredibly slow. Another's early hyperactivity may take a more unacceptable form now in episodes of violence — unrestrained rage that takes itself out on people as well as on unsuspecting doors and dishes. In a way, the person with this problem seems to "pass" in society most successfully. He may wear black leather and develop a "punk" style, very macho.

By this time, I'm into the grey area every parent has feared since the problem child was tiny. Here he is, all grown up, with no place to go, no job, no future. What's going to become of him? Until very recently, these young people had no labels and no help. Now they have labels. I'm not sure if that's progress.

Whatever their title, the young adults like Matthew who are now in their early twenties are often the ones whose problems were undiagnosed when they were younger. Now, at least in the elementary schools, there is some haphazard attempt at recognition of them, though still not much is done. (What's more, money for special education is the first to disappear when times are tight.)

The young women have slipped through the system, by and large. If they're lucky and have a reasonable amount of hand-eye coordination, they have learned to cook, perhaps to sew, and have developed some life skills. They have learned to be meek and friendly, sociable and quiet, and remain at home with their parents. Depending on the extent of their problem and their own attitudes, they have managed to find jobs as unskilled workers. Or else they remain at home, helping out. Smart mothers have taught them to cook and clean; others have kept them virtual children, wrapped in a cocoon of misguided love.

The young men are another story. What they do depends on the range and extent of their disability. Parental pressure and persistence have kept some in school, some kind of school, and although the choices and opportunities are meagre, there are still places for them to go, most of them expensive. Others, with more severe damage, are in sheltered workshops, learning some kind of make-work job, and there is now in most provinces some kind of follow-up and guarantee that they will continue to find employment, however simple and menial and however small the wage. Others are unemployed. Of these, some still live at home, still supported and excused by a long-suffering family. Others beat up on their mothers and sisters long ago and drifted out. These are the ones who look like tough punks, who appear to have made a choice to drop out. Did they ever really have a choice?

I know a number of young men, all around my son's age, but each has a slightly different problem and each has a very different solution. When I say "solution," I don't mean a way of solving the problem. There are no answers at this stage, there are merely stopgaps, attempts to find something to do, something to fill the time while waiting for the future to begin.

One young man is in a sheltered workshop. He is high-functioning, as they say, can do all his own shopping, make his own decisions. He lives at home and has a girlfriend. Another, more skilled, has a job in a hardware store and lives in a tiny apartment with his new wife. Another, still at home, is struggling through yet another institution of learning that his parents hope will bring him to some level of academic skill where he can get a job. He is personable but frightened. He won't see his friends and makes promises he doesn't keep.

I say "friends," but do you realize how few friends most of these young people have? They have never gone through a school system that provided them with the automatic camaraderie of the playground or the long-term association that most people call friendship. They've never had comfortable continuity or proximity with their peers, having usually gone out of their neighbourhood to special classes, or having been shunted from one attempted solution to another. When did they ever have a chance to make friends?

Another young man works for his father in his paint store. Another one is trying to make it in a community college, still trying to prove to his parents that he will succeed. He's quite competent, actually, but he's awkward and shy and clumsy and fearful. Another one is sitting in his bedroom, defeated. His parents have divorced, mostly because of their tensions over him. He has run through the school system and has retreated into bouts of schizophrenia and depression. Every once in a while he beats up his mother and sister and is given a respite (for whom?) in a short-term holding tank for behavioural problems.

And what of Matthew? By the fall of 1980, he was living at home and had returned to the Haney Centre, taking extra tutorial lessons in reading (at my expense) to compensate for the lack of academic work at the school. But he was still learning things.

One day I asked him, "What did you learn today?"

"Shapes," he said. "Triangles, circles, squares."

I was shocked; that was kindergarten stuff. But it wasn't. It was a lesson in laundry. Matt had learned the guide to the washing instructions that appear in the labels of most clothes today. I was impressed. You keep forgetting, you see, you keep taking for granted, that everyone knows about simple things like laundry instructions. No, everyone doesn't. It still has to be spelled out.

Matt was also becoming completely adept at the transit system. One morning a week the students were told to come in with a transfer from such-and-such a subway station, chosen at random from anywhere in the city. Matt knew his way around most of Toronto, better than I did. He still wasn't very good at making change (neither am I). He was a long way from long division, but his social skills were terrific. He had even met a girl, but that's another chapter.

He seemed to be serene and stable, as far as his mental health was concerned. He was completely off the Haldol. He had suffered a mild seizure one hot summer day following a twenty-four-hour 'flu bug (still calling for his father during his moments of anguish). His problem was me.

I had run out of backup. I was travelling more and more in the course of my work, and finding fewer and fewer ways to take care of Matthew in my absence. While he had been in the boarding school, this had not been a problem. When Kate returned home from her travels and lived with me till she built up her stake and found work, this had not been a problem. While John lived at home during the summer and worked in Toronto, this had not been a problem. But the fall of 1980 presented a problem. I had been commissioned by the United Church to write a book, a collection of twenty interviews with people all across Canada. I had to go to the people, to meet them and talk to them, and they lived in every province from British Columbia to Newfoundland. I would be gone for several weeks, and then I planned to go away to write the book. I had a very tight deadline and I had to retreat from the beguiling pressures of working where I live.

I tried my sister-in-law. Bless her! I didn't ask often, but when I did, she took Matt in without question. The only problem was that she lived out of Toronto, so far out that it wasn't even suburban. Matt had to take a train into town every morning and then the transit to his school at the west end of the city. He was condemned to about four hours of travelling time each day, too hard to sustain for long. And it was too much to ask of my sister-in-law very often. I waited for emergencies, tried every other resource before I turned to her.

I had always held the idea of group homes in the back of my mind, from the time I first heard of them, when Matt was much younger. The idea of a separate establishment and an opportunity to develop some independence and learn some life skills seemed to be a wonderful solution to the problem faced by people who can't live alone. By this time in Toronto there was a system in place. I searched out the names and began to ask for help.

The only trouble with any wonderful idea is that there isn't enough of it to go around. The Metropolitan Toronto Association for the Mentally Retarded (MTAMR), which runs the group homes I had my hopes pinned on, had a waiting list as long as your arm. I told them about my situation and Matt's, explaining that he was epileptic and couldn't be left alone, even if he could manage by himself; that his mother was a working widow who had to travel for her work; that my current absence would be followed by others. Stopgap solutions would not do.

But that was what I was offered at first, a stopgap. There was a large group home, a relief home for short-term residents. The relief was for the parents of m.r. people, providing a home for their child when the family needed a holiday. These clients, not necessarily young, were quite severely retarded, often noisy and disoriented, unable to sustain a conversation let alone coherent activity. Matthew hated the place, but there was no other choice, it seemed.

Still, I tried. By this time I had completed the western leg of my "spiritual journey," as one of my associates called it. I had a longer trip to the Maritimes facing me. My employers were worried that I wasn't going to be able to get away. Now I'll tell you something that's a little hard to believe. My employers, all United Church ministers, had trouble believing it, too. A little background information might help.

In Catherine Marshall's book *A Man Called Peter*, she describes a time in her life when she was very sick. Unless she got help, which she could ill afford, she was going to have to spend a year in a convalescent hospital, unable to care for her husband and son. Ordinary channels provided no solution; there seemed to be no alternative to a dreaded separation from her family. So she prayed for help. And one day the doorbell rang and a woman stood there saying she understood that Mrs. Marshall needed someone to help her.

I did that. I did it in Stratford. The fall that Kate left home to go to university, the boys were too young to leave alone and I was going in and out of Toronto a lot, only a night or two at a time, but too long for them to be left. I couldn't afford a sitter to cover my absences, nor was a full-time sitter the right answer. John was too old for that, even if too young for complete independence. So I prayed.

And the phone rang, and a public health nurse was telling me that she was saving up to go to Europe and would be willing to live with me for free room and board in return for her presence during my absence. Then, when she was ready to leave for Europe, a friend wrote me from British Columbia that a friend of her daughter's needed a place to stay while she "found herself" — not as happy a solution, as it turned out, but a necessary one.

I told my minister friends this story and assured them that something would turn up. We had to focus a little prayer on the subject, that was all. Just a few days before I was due to leave, when I was really beginning to wonder what I would do if something/body didn't turn up, my phone rang.

It was a friend of John's, "passing by," he said, hoping to see John. He knew, he said later, that in all probability John would be back at university (he was). But Chris was downtown when the urge to call on John came over him and though his home was way out in the suburbs and it was getting late, he decided for some reason to walk to my place (close to the downtown area, but a half-hour walk, nonetheless), and say hello. When I told him John wasn't there, he asked if he could come up anyway. Chris was studying forestry, and was alternating between study and work units. I had thought he was on a work phase, but discovered in the course of our conversation that he was back in classes at the University of Toronto. The light dawned. My apartment was closer to the downtown campus than his family home; he might not be adverse to the idea. And I would pay him.

"I don't suppose you'd consider living with Matt while I'm away on an assignment," I said.

"Yes," said Chris. "I would."

"Well, you were meant to come," I said.

"I wondered why I was walking over here," he said.

Listen, you don't use this power to find parking places. God is not a parking-lot attendant. But in cases of special need....

My minister friends shook their heads, too.

But that, also, was a short-term solution, and there were problems, as it turned out, though they had nothing to do with Chris. So I kept on phoning my contact at MTAMR and asking her when Matt could get into a group home. She knew more about my activities than my kids did at that point.

"Believe me, Mrs. Wylie," she said one day in a weary voice, "we're trying. Everyone is getting very tired of hearing the name Matthew Wylie."

So that's how Matt got into a group home. Parents of problem children become very good naggers. Persistence is all. Well, it's not all, but it helps. It also helps that people on the other end are sympathetic and compassionate.

The next problem was practical and pressing. How was I going to pay for this group home? I couldn't afford to keep two homes. Doreen Crystal, the principal at Haney, ever helpful, had told me that Matt might qualify for a disability pension. He was going to be twenty in a few months, and though he was still at school, a school paid for by the Toronto School Board, God knew what he was going to do next, and He hadn't told me yet. So I phoned around, got the information and the forms, and applied. And was turned down. Good advice and encouragement from Doreen Crystal made me persevere. I applied for a review. We were given an appointment several weeks hence, and Doreen Crystal briefed me.

There is a key question in the application form, I discovered, that must be answered correctly in order for the applicant to qualify for a disability pension. I hadn't answered it correctly the first time; that's why Matt was turned down. At the hearing, I was told that I was far too optimistic, that my hope that Matt would one day live an independent life with some measure of confident autonomy was unreasonable. If the board could be convinced that his was a hopeless case, then he would qualify.

Next time I answered the form correctly. Matt was hopeless, I agreed, and would never be employable. Now he qualified. All we had to lose was pride.

The first pension cheque arrived just before a room became available in a group home. I should mention a couple of things about the pension. First, it is designed to keep one supported, but not lavishly, and the provincial government doesn't like to see thrift in the recipients. No one is allowed to have more than $1,500 in savings. If he does, his pension will be cut off. (A Family Benefit Allowance worker checks every once in a while.) Also, he is not allowed to receive money from other sources. If he does, his pension is cut by that amount. I kept trying to tell "them" that Matt was receiving an Orphans' Allowance (he's half an orphan, but Canada Pension calls him an orphan). It took a while to register, but when it finally did, his pension was cut by the other amount he was receiving. Matt actually earned a little money one summer, working as a junior counsellor at a Y day camp. This job had to be discussed with the FBA worker, to make sure the salary did not exceed the acceptable limit. It didn't—nowhere close.

So it would be wise to set up an irrevocable trust in your will if you have a child on such a pension. That way you can leave money to your son (or daughter) and the government will still not take away the pension. Assign one of your other adult children, if you have one, or another relative to act as trustee to administer the money for the benefit of your heir. You should have two other trustees outside of the family, perhaps your accountant or lawyer and a close, trusted family friend. The small amount of money I will leave Matt would certainly never be sufficient to support him, but it could provide him with the occasional vacation or a new television set or some luxury he might not otherwise enjoy.

The whole set of machinery we had set in motion seemed to be working smoothly. Matt would have a new home and a means of paying for it. He also, though I didn't realize it at the time, gained another family and a whole network of support, something neither of us had enjoyed since his father died.

Let me tell you how wonderful group homes are. Matthew has learned to do his own banking, pay his bills, and handle money. He even has to file an income-tax return, though his counsellor helps him with that, and all he does is sign his name (that's all I do, too, but I pay an accountant for the privilege). He rotates the cleaning chores with his fellow residents, and has really learned how to keep house.

One time he came home for a weekend when I was chained to the typewriter, madly trying to finish an assignment to meet a deadline. He looked around the apartment with disgust and commented, "This place is filthy," got out the vacuum cleaner and vacuumed the living room for me. That kind of criticism I welcome!

He has learned how to cook, and cooks dinner one night a week for himself and his buddies, including the staff (who guide). He also fends for himself on the weekends that he stays at his group home. (He usually comes to me when I'm in town.) The preparation of the food includes the planning and shopping for it. He does his own laundry, changes his own sheets, runs his own errands, like getting his hair cut, or picking up library books. (Books on cassettes are available through library services for people who are not skilled readers, by the way. A doctor's signature is all that is required to plug them into a service most people think is reserved for the blind.) In addition, though he might not have chosen them or even discovered them by himself, he counts as friends—more like family—the people with whom he lives: Betsy, who is only a couple of years older than he is, like one of his sisters; friendly Lillian, who is only a few years younger than I am and who talks more than I do; John and Steve, whom I do not know yet, because they are newcomers, replacing Bruce and Barry who qualified for the apartment program (the advanced phase of group-home living) and who have set up housekeeping for themselves now, with some continuing but less obtrusive guidance from the MTAMR support system.

Matt, too, has gained the support of that system, in the form of counsellors and guides, who tell me what to do, too, and who are unfailingly helpful and watchful, to say nothing of innovative, imaginative, friendly, and caring. I can't tell you how comforting it is to be able to discuss Matt, his plans, his problems, and his future with someone else, particularly when that someone is equipped and trained to help, and has knowledge of and access to programs and aids I wouldn't even know about. It was Matt's dear counsellor Ellen Overton who discovered Kohai Educational Centre for us, the best school he ever attended. She has moved on now, away from Matt's group home, and we both still miss her.

A lot of parents are afraid to put their problem child out of their home and into a group home for fear of—what? That they will be accused of neglecting their child. That they will accuse themselves of neglecting their child, and they can't bear the burden of guilt that would lay on them. That the child would suffer. That he wouldn't be as well taken care of. That no one will ever understand the child as well as his own family. That the child would feel rejected.

But let's face it, he is no longer a child. His parents aren't getting any younger. What's going to become of him when the parents are too old to care for him, or when they die? Then what? Then you have a middle-aged, helpless human being flailing around, too old to adjust happily to a new environment, and scarcely competent in any of the simple skills of living. That's care? That isn't even love.

But I can understand the reluctance and fear, because I went through them myself. What kind of mother was I, with a perfectly good home and space to spare for Matthew, to shove him out among strangers? A busy one, for starters. I had other needs, besides my need to care for Matt, and they were more pressing—like money. It took a dear, blunt friend, though, to ease my mind of a possible guilt trip.

She said that, ironically, both Matt and I had benefited from my husband's death. Matt was forced to become more independent, and I was allowed not to feel guilty about it, because I had to earn my living. I can't think of any rebuttal to that. Irony is very hard to assimilate.

Anyway, the move was made. By the time this book is published, Matt will have been in his group home for three years. It took over a year and a half before he started referring to it as home, and then not consistently. In a way, he has two homes now. But I am assured that when my home shrinks, as it must when I grow too old and incompetent to cope with this space, he will still have a home to call his own.

A number of different organizations operate group homes in the country. Not all the homes are for handicapped people. Some are for ex-mental patients, some for ex-prisoners, and some now for battered, runaway wives. Harder even than finding space in the homes, whose waiting lists far exceed available accommodation, is overcoming community attitudes to them.

I like to think that people are essentially kind. I'd like to believe that the uniform resistance to group homes in the midst of a "normal" neighbourhood exists only because people are ill informed about them. They are afraid that the occupants will be noisy and strange, that they will urinate on their front lawns, or rape their daughters, or let the place run to seed.

When my son John was at university, he lived for a couple of years in a townhouse with four or five other young men – in other words, a group home. Their hygiene and housekeeping methods were rudimentary. They didn't clean the place, they "shovelled it out," as John put it. When the dishes towered in the sink, they would take a look at the mess of food-covered plates and comment, "That either has to be fed or washed." If a social worker had checked up on them, they would have been condemned, along with the house. But they were considered "normal" and no one ever checked up on them, except an occasional visiting mother. At which point they hid the mess.

No group home for special adults would ever be allowed to run like that. These homes are subject to constant care, surveillance, guidance, inspection, and maintenance. The occupants keep their homes cleaner than you do, in all probability. Gardens are planted, lawns are cut, walks are shovelled, walls (both inside and out) are painted. The houses are in better shape, usually, than their neighbouring ones. So much for property values.

Supervision is constant. The inhabitants of a group home are not allowed to be unproductively occupied. Though each one has a key to the house in case he or she gets sick and must go home to bed, that is for emergency use only. The staff goes away each morning and so must the occupants: to work, to school, to day care, to training or sheltered workshops, therapy, whatever. When they return, they have their chores to do – the cooking, cleaning, and so on. They're too busy to bug their neighbours.

One young man, a fellow resident of Matt's, used to love to practise basketball in the driveway at the side of the house, throwing his ball into a hoop attached above the garage door. A neighbour complained of the noise of the bouncing ball. Ellen, the counsellor, and Barry discussed the problem with the neighbour, and agreed on acceptable times for basketball practice. This happens with "normal" nieghbours, too. I can remember we used to have a neighbour who, it seemed to us, made a point of power-mowing the lawn whenever we had guests for an outdoor barbecue. But that neighbour wasn't handicapped; he was just ornery.

As for the possibility of unsuitable or violent behaviour, I think these fears are wild and unjustified. Handicapped people are usually gentle and often defeated; they're not looking for more trouble or rejection. Ex-mental patients are locked into chemical straitjackets – the psychotropic drugs that enable them to function outside an institution. When they do reach the end of their psychotropic tether, they usually do more harm to themselves than to anyone else. And the last thing a former prisoner wants to do is go back to jail. All these people are human beings and deserve a chance to live in a decent, accepting neighbourhood. Remember the little girl's line: "A stranger is a friend I haven't met yet." These people are our friends. They are also our children – mine, anyway.

Right now, there aren't enough group homes to go around, and the lack of them may become drastic. Run by several different organizations across the country, with separate board structures and different sources of funding, all these homes may disappear if narrow-minded ratepayers' associations have their way. In the meantime, governments are cutting their costs where they think money doesn't matter – in spending on education, health care, and social services.

So group homes may get lost in the shuffle. As I write this, the government of Ontario is going through with a plan to close the smaller residences for the mentally retarded, claiming to be arranging placement in smaller group homes. But the homes aren't materializing, and far too many lost human beings are in the process of being shoved into the huge, impersonal institutions that provide custodial care only, often geographically removed from community or family support, and with little or no attempt at education or training of any kind. It's a pity—something governments are short of these days.

Pity, or, better, compassion, may be in short supply in governments these days, but I continue to find it in individuals. I trust there are enough caring people to make life livable for the handicapped. If there aren't enough group homes to go around, there must be alternatives, humane ones, to enable the developmentally handicapped to live decently. I just came across a very humane alternative: circle groups.

Call such a group a committee, a network, or a circle, it's a cluster of caring people who take on the responsibility for a handicapped person. This group may be comprised of family members, friends, or concerned people who are simply looking for a one-on-one method of voluntary human service. You don't have to go to the Third World to find helpless people to help; there are lots of them right here. Circles are one imaginative way of helping them.

Circles have mostly grown out of parents' casual support groups meeting in church basements or private living rooms and developing into an unorganized underground movement, each of them dealing with a specific case. One I heard of went so far as to be designated in a will. I'll tell you about it because the case illustrates how a circle works.

The parents of a handicapped son have named in their will each of the people helping him, citing each persons' particular responsibility with regard to their grown child. Someone looks after the money (see irrevocable trust, page 148); someone is adept at dealing with the government red tape that wraps community support systems; another watches the clothing needs; someone else takes care of recreation, and so on. This group is already in existence and meets regularly to see to the needs of its ward.

Another group I heard of has enabled a young woman, confined to a wheelchair with muscular dystrophy, not only to cope with her life but to do it with a fair measure of independence in a living accommodation of her own. She named her group the Joshua

Committee because they have helped her to break down the walls between her and society, between her and a normal life.

Even lacking such sophisticated and dedicated support, handicapped people across the country can benefit from parent or family support groups. So can the families and parents. As with any other anxiety, it helps to know it is shared, that other people face similar problems, and have found ways of coping with them.

That's what everyone needs — someone who cares.

CHAPTER FOURTEEN

SEX

This is where we separate the men from the boys, and both from the women. But how do you separate them? With the sexual emphasis of contemporary society it is impossible to ignore sex and the external demands it places on the individual – to say nothing of the internal ones already imposed by nature. "In the spring a young man's fancy turns"... to what the girl has been thinking about all winter. And summer and fall. Old joke.

Matt has a good, healthy libido. I can tell by the way he notices girls, talks about them, and enjoys sexual innuendoes in the movies and on television (so do I). His camp counsellors told me that he always had a way with the girls, too, and that when it came to teaming up for projects, Matt usually won a couple of the prize girls to join him in the activity. He could talk to them, he could listen, and perhaps best of all, he was a gentle boy and didn't present a threat. But that's a long way from the next step, from pairing off and dating.

If special kids have trouble making friends among their normal peers because of their separation from average childhood and adolescent society, how much more difficult it is for them to have friends of the opposite sex. Not only the lack of easy, casual opportunity but their own hang-ups hinder them. Their sense of failure and inferiority, their shyness, their fear of rejection, all conspire now to make them tongue-tied and reticent around girls. Then, too, they seldom have very much money, another prerequisite these days before one can have an active social life with males or females.

Matt's brother John earned money of his own from the time he was twelve years old, when he signed winter contracts with neighbours to keep their driveways clear, using our snowblower. From the time his father died when he was fourteen, he earned his own allowance, bought his own clothes, split the fees of his summer camp with me, and put himself through university. My daughters did the same thing (though less easily; as females they earned less money than John). I used to joke wryly that there's nothing like a death in the family to bring out the character in one's children. The point is that normal achievers have a fighting chance to make some discretionary money. Handicapped kids don't have that opportunity. The only gratuitous, external (that is, from a source other than his own family) money Matt ever had outside the Christmas and birthday monetary gifts from aunts or his Big Brother, was twenty-five dollars he was paid for a television appearance and the small stipend for junior counselling services at Y day camp. Oh, and he had a short-lived job walking a dog for neighbours while the man recovered from surgery (at a dollar a walk). He had an allowance from me to cover his transportation and incidental expenses, usually entertainment, such as movies. But he didn't have a lot of money, certainly not much to spend on girls, and I think that's typical of kids like him.

So that's another social handicap as far as boy-girl relationships are concerned — not as bad today as it used to be, of course, because kids split their expenses or take turns treating each other, far more than they did when I was a girl. (So do grown-ups. It's not so much a reflection of the feminist movement as it is of the economic times.)

But where do they find the girls? They go to school out of their neighbourhood, and the school itself is a special school, isolated from the big social melting-pots where boy usually meets girl. Well, of course, they find them at their own school. And that's what happened in the fall of 1980. A new girl showed up at the Haney Centre. For Matt, it was love at first sight.

Suddenly the conversation at home was full of Sandy (not her real name). She was, according to Matt, lovely, witty, friendly, a real charmer. Matt started coming home later and later after school because he would take Sandy for coffee afterwards. For Sandy he learned to smoke, and he bought her cigarettes as well as his own. I wasn't fully aware of the changes this attachment would make in Matt's life for some time (I've already described my writing assignment that fall). Nor did it change Matt's life that much immediately. Since he was at his aunt's and then at the big relief home, his freedom of movement was more restricted than it would have been if he had been living at home steadily. But when he was home, he began to spend most of his free time on the weekend at Sandy's place, often staying for lunch or supper; going shopping with her; taking her, and sometimes a younger sister, to the movies or roller-skating; and, I gather, learning about sex. Sandy may have been slow, but not in everything. Matt was utterly beguiled.

I finally invited this paragon for dinner one weekend when I was home. What did I expect? I knew she was a pupil at Haney, therefore, at least somewhat mentally retarded. I knew nothing of her background, but she gave it away as soon as she opened her mouth.

Because Sandy was a simple girl, her ploys were touchingly transparent to me. They were like caricatures of things she had seen and heard in the movies and on television. But they worked. She would say something like "Matthew, you're a prince," a tribute that brighter girls would choke on. But Matthew would beam at her and visibly grow two inches as he added princely stature to his frame. Sandy made him feel good about himself, and isn't that still one of the secrets of female success with men? There's a line of Jessamyn West's I am reminded of: "Men ain't got any heart for courting a girl they can't pass—let alone catch up with." Even as we enter the third decade of feminism, it's still true, true, true.

So Matthew had found a girl he could keep up with and pass—in a manner of speaking. She had it all over him in street smarts. She was giving him a tactile education, I gather, that he had been totally deprived of thus far in his life. Sex had reared its lovely head. Matt couldn't stay away.

Nor did her family try to keep him away. For one thing, they were much more casual about living arrangements than we had ever been. Once that winter Sandy had to go to hospital for several stitches to her bottom, because she had sat heavily on a butcher knife on the living-room sofa. (What was a butcher knife *doing* on the living-room sofa?) Mealtimes, I gathered, were haphazard, as were the menus, and they were usually preceded by a trip to the store to get the essentials (sometimes provided by Matthew). Still, Matt enjoyed it. I think he had missed the easy give-and-take of family life. He and I were alone now. Life was much more interesting over at Sandy's where there were lots of people and activities and often a close association of adults and children. Parties were spontaneous and inclusive and no one seemed to pay any attention to time or tomorrow.

One night Matt was later than usual. A friend and I had gone to a movie, and he came in for a nightcap. Matt wasn't home, late as it was, and didn't appear while we were having our drink. I couldn't raise anyone by phone at Sandy's house. So my friend insisted on helping me find Matt. We drove to Sandy's and found out from an upstairs neighbour where the family had gone for a party. By the time we got there — at nearly three o'clock in the morning — the party had spilled out onto the street. I spoke to Sandy's father, one of the people reeling in the road, introduced myself and asked for Matthew. Matt came staggering across the street, happy (very happy) with the party and not at all pleased to see us. We took him home, where he was sick to his stomach. I was terrified that he was going to have a seizure. (He didn't.)

I had asked Sandy's father several key questions: how did they think Matt was going to get home after the subways stopped running? He said the kid could have stayed over with them. I asked when were they going to let me know that? He said they were going to phone me any minute. I told him Matt was unable to drink because of the drugs he was on, and asked what he had been drinking. He didn't think Matt had been drinking at all, maybe a few sips of someone else's beer.

I was beginning to learn what I was dealing with — a whole different set of standards. With my sheltered background, I had never encountered this before. Matthew's handicap keeps taking me out into the real world — not a bad thing. I am not only learning street smarts myself, I am also learning tolerance. Nevertheless, I was still intent on protecting my child. I phoned Sandy's mother the next day and told her of Matt's epilepsy and his inability to combine Dilantin with alcohol. I suggested that if they gave him liquor again I would be forced to call the police. I had never threatened anyone in my life before, and I was ashamed of myself. I needn't have been. The family was soon ready to threaten me.

I went off to my hideaway to write my book, and our friend Chris stayed with Matthew. For the first time in his life, Matt had curfews laid down for him. I guess they always existed, but there had never been the need to spell them out or enforce them before. I pointed out that common courtesy demanded that a person say goodbye when leaving the house and give some estimate of time of return; that when a person is delayed, it is customary to phone and let others at home know of that delay and the reason for it, and that there are reasonable times at which one might expect someone home at night. You think your child has learned these rules by osmosis, but no. As with everything else, all information must be spelled out. It's like Jean Kerr's rule in her book *Please Don't Eat the Daisies*. *After* the kids ate the daisies in her centrepiece for a dinner party, she always remembered to tell them not to.

Now, about sex. This is where Matt and I both missed his father. The boarding-school director had told me several years earlier that it was very evident from Matt's behaviour patterns that he had been raised largely by a woman and had very little contact with men. He also told me that although they offered some sex education in the school, I had better have a long talk with Matt. So I did, on several occasions. The first time I remember was rather funny. I mean, it's harder than it used to be to tell your child about sex and how wonderful it is and how careful you have to be about its indiscriminate use because these days there's such a lot of it around and few people, it seems, wait until marriage to enjoy it. But I said nice things about appropriate ages and the right time and to everything there is a season and all that, and Matt cut in.

"What about Mrs. Robinson?" he asked. He had just seen *The Graduate* on television. Right. And he knew I was dating and he must have wondered about me.

But then, with Sandy a reality in Matt's life and the real thing happening to him — no more vicarious thrills from the late movie — I had to start worrying about responsibility. I was slow to realize this. The broken curfews made me aware that the dim, idealized future I had talked about with Matt was upon us. My daughters phoned me at my retreat and said I had better come home early. Matt was ignoring his curfews, disobeying Chris, and Sandy's family was threatening a shotgun marriage. So I came home. (Fortunately, I had finished my book.)

I never did find out whether or not Sandy had had her tubes tied. I got conflicting stories, second-hand, dependent on her mood. Throughout the winter, I heard, via Matt, that she had had a baby and had been sterilized after that—no, that was her cousin, she said later. Then she said she would be going to hospital to have it done, and there were hospital visits, in addition to the bottom-stitching incident, but it was never clear what for. Whatever the truth was, in the fall of 1980, when I came rushing home to cries and grievances from her family that Matt had ravished their child and must make an honest woman of her, the claim was that Sandy could, indeed, have children and that Matt might well become a father.

I took a family friend with me to have a chat with Sandy's family, a father-figure who could play the heavy for me if necessary. We had to go unannounced because the phone had been disconnected for non-payment. No one was home. When the telephone service was restored, I had my chat with Sandy's mother over the phone, and somehow I talked her out of the idea that Matt was going to be the family's meal ticket. But if I stopped their speculation, I had only just begun mine.

I had been so busy worrying about Matt's schooling, about his role in society, about his living quarters and his future, that I had lost sight of his real future as a human being. I had always entertained the idea of Matt marrying. He is such a lovable human being, and needs so much love that marriage seems to me to be an entirely acceptable state for him. But again I had been romanticizing some rosy, distant future and not thinking about present reality at all. Here was reality. Marriage I could accept, but fatherhood? We had to have a chat. Again.

"I think we should talk to Dr. Taylor about a vasectomy," I said to Matt.

"Do you mean I can never be a father?" he asked me.

"I think you'd make a wonderful uncle," I said, "but not a father," I said. "Let's talk about it."

So we talked, and I considered aloud for him the cost of fatherhood, the price of haircuts and clothes and lessons, to say nothing of shelter and food and furniture, and all the responsibilities of family life. How did he propose to pay for all that? Then, too, there was the never-ending care and responsibility for an infant and the need to watch over a little one and anticipate both hazards and needs. Sadly, Matt could see my point.

I have observed since that these kids talk a lot about marriage. It seems to be the ultimate badge of acceptance and adulthood, society's recognition that they are truly grown-up. Again, sometimes, when I hear them talking, it sounds like a caricature, like some kind of out-of-sync parroting of adult talk. Only instead of saying, "When I grow up" they say, "When I get married."

Marie Putnam is a young m.r. woman who has written a book called *Mentely Handicapped Love*. Here is an excerpt:

> I love Doug so much now, he love me too. We walk together on the street last week. He kiss me on the lips now.
> I got new book now.
> Doug wanted me to married me now. I say yes and waited!
> Mother wanted to do dishes now.
> I love to see him now.
> Oh, you can't cooked said me.

It's touching, and frightening. Frightening because one fears for them. Why shouldn't they have such expectations? Why can't we make it possible for them to have companionship and a lifelong partner? (I am probably being romantic again, but I have a feeling that such liaisons might be more lasting than marriage among the so-called normies.)

But I had a lot to learn and think about. I did have a talk with Dr. Taylor. He agreed with my attitude then and promised to side with me if I had any trouble over the fact that Matthew was still under twenty-one.

Recently, I spoke to him again, telling him of my revised estimate and doubts. "You know in your heart what's right," said Taylor. "Deep down you know whether your child can handle it." We cluck about children having children – all the teenage unwed mothers hanging on to their real-live dolls, but we haven't given nearly enough thought to the permanent children in our society and what their roles and rights are.

The more I find out, the deeper and fuller becomes the can of worms I have opened. I can't figure out the moral imperatives of the problems raised. We have to consider sterilization, birth control, and abortion. And then we have to talk about child neglect and child abuse. And then we have to talk about human freedom and choice. It's all so big, it's another book, but maybe I can offer a few thoughts.

I met a woman a few years ago who had a mentally retarded daughter, then about thirty-five years old. The daughter was a sweet, helpful woman, skilled in homemaking, thanks to her mother's training. She had a boyfriend, a man her own age, also mentally retarded, and they planned to be married soon — no rush. Her mother had searched her own soul deeply and, after many discussions with her daughter, had watched as the daughter signed the necessary papers of consent (this was in British Columbia) and went through with the sterilization. But though it was the daugher's hand that had held the pen, the mother knew very well that it was her will that had guided that hand, and she was overcome with guilt and doubt. Had she done the right thing, or had she denied her daughter the joys of motherhood? Had she denied a child the right to be born?

No one has solved these problems. The argument rages on about women's right to control their own bodies. On the one hand, the pro-abortionists are saying that a woman should have the choice whether or not to bear a child, and that an unwanted child is the one who suffers child abuse and becomes, in many cases, a further burden on society. On the other hand, the right-to-lifers are saying that every foetus has the right to be born. Now go back a bit. In the case of the mentally handicapped, does every human being have the right to decide whether he/she has the right to have a child? You may have thought this was solely a feminist issue, and so did I, until I talked to Matthew. He does not want to be denied the right to fatherhood.

But what about the rights and the future of a child born to m.r. parents? It is perfectly possible for such parents to have a normal child, that is, one with a normal intelligence. I have heard of such children who rapidly become their parents' keeper, being smarter than they are. That is, if they live that long. People who scarcely know how to look after themselves don't know much about looking after babies. They forget to move pots full of hot soup so that the handles turn in and can't be pulled over to scald an inquisitive, exploring child. They forget to lock protective gates at the top of stairs so that a toddler doesn't fall down. They don't know much about nutrition, and can't understand why a child doesn't thrive on Kool-Aid instead of milk. They don't know how to handle a simple cut so that it doesn't get infected, or diarrhea so that the child doesn't dehydrate. And apart from the physical care, which is crucial, they don't know how to stimulate a child so that it will be ready for school, or life.

I was on a public commission investigating the effects of financial cutbacks in the mental health care system of the province of Ontario a few years ago. I was surprised to learn that there actually is an organization in Toronto designed to give some sort of intellectual stimulus to children of mentally handicapped parents. The program, ideally, is supposed to begin when a child is three or four months old, but it is woefully underfunded and understaffed and there is a waiting list far beyond anything they can realistically cope with. But at least someone has recognized the problem. There must be similar programs elsewhere in Canada, and I suspect they are similarly short of money.

But this is what I was worried about when I suggested to Matthew that he was better equipped to be an uncle than a father. And yet....

What about love? What about freedom? I heard of a young m.r. couple who couldn't cope with their tiny little girl. She was a mass of bruises and cuts, not from child abuse but from accidents her parents weren't smart enough to prevent. When the Children's Aid Society finally took the baby away from the parents, they were upset, hurt, bewildered. Why had someone taken their beloved child from them? How can you answer that? The older I get, the more I can see both sides of every question, and the less capable I am of making a decision. The answer to such a situation lies not in separating parent and child, but in training the parents and making the child safe. Unfortunately, such humane methods are slow and expensive. Society prefers instant answers, even if they're not really answers.

Pat Capponi is a social-change agent, an advocate, if you will, living and working in the Parkdale area in Toronto, where she is supervisor of PARC, the drop-in centre for the ex-mental patients in which the area abounds. Herself an ex-mental patient, she has a deep understanding and endless compassion for the problems of these people. She is also having to develop some knowledge and understanding of m.r. people, as more and more of them have begun to use PARC. She tells me that between 30 and 40 per cent of the people who show up at PARC now are mentally handicapped.

PARC provides not only the facilities of a downtown club, with cheap coffee, newspapers and magazines, pool, crafts, and activities, but also awareness programs and a platform for the disadvantaged and ignored ex-mental patients to make themselves heard without fear of reprisal. In the fall of 1983, for example, they flocked to participate in a debate about abortion.

The pro-life representative was outrageous, according to Pat, totally irrational, emotional, and deaf to arguments. But all the PARC members supported her for one simple reason. If they favoured abortion, they would lose their children, and they want them. Not only that, if their parents had supported abortion, they might not be here.

The same is true in the case of sterilization of the mentally unfit. If these people's parents had been sterilized, they wouldn't exist. Never mind whether society wants them, or what their lives are like. Life is sweet. Life is also to be revered. Any kind of genetic programming smacks of master-racism. Who, indeed, has the right to choose who will be born? And who is worth saving? If George Bernard Shaw's theories about genetic selection had been practised, the playwright himself would never have been born. His parents were certainly unsuitable, but look what they produced!

The pro-lifers are short-sighted, nonetheless. They are so concerned with getting that foetus born that they neglect to consider the life a disadvantaged child faces. An ideal society, where everyone is cared for, is very expensive. It costs the have's a lot to care for the have-not's. We are an essentially selfish society today. We do not seem to be willing to make any sacrifices for others. What others need is empathy, gentleness, and care. Those are the things we seem least willing to give.

And what of the feminist movement's claim that a woman has a right to control her own body? Mentally retarded women also want the right to control their lives: they want the right to have a child of their own. And as soon as you've said that, you have to ask, what about the rights of the child, once it is born? Oh, dear.

Black-and-white, yes-or-no decisions are the easy way out. Life isn't easy; no one ever said it was. Some of the choices we think we have the right to make are ridiculous. I like what Margaret Mead said about abortion: given our present backward state of development, abortion is a necessary evil. When society improves, it will no longer be necessary.

As it is now, we tolerate no differences, make no allowances for weakness. We want to hide the klutzes and the misfits. Now we're trying to make sure that they never get born. Isn't it time someone started talking about the quality of life? *Life*.

But I return to the personal, specific question: does Matthew have the right to be a father? Could he ever handle fatherhood? I don't know. But I think that he must be granted the choice, and that I have no right to make it for him. Of course, as soon as you use the word choice, you must also use the word responsibility. Responsibility means taking action for one's self; it means being informed and participating in one's own life, rather than passively accepting society's impositions and denials. One of the methods of such participation is, of course, birth control. Not abortion or sterilization, but a conscious, wise use of birth control that puts the reins of power into the hands of the individual. Pat Capponi says that people can be taught. They can learn to take normal, sensible precautions. It may take longer to explain before they understand the *why* as well as the *how*, but it can be done. This is before-the-fact behaviour, much more reasoned than after-the-fact violence, such as abortion, or, even later, after-the-fact neglect or child abuse.

If I had been told before he was born that Matthew would be damaged, would I have chosen to have him? Yes. And whatever his difficulties have been, he, too, would choose to be here. I know, because I asked him.

CHAPTER FIFTEEN

THE FUTURE

"I was thinking," said Matt one day several years ago, "how different my life would be if I had a better brain." He was very calm as he said it; there was no self-pity in his voice. He had long since assimilated the hard fact of his handicap. Still, if he had his druthers, he'd rather be normal. He made me think of the Scarecrow in *The Wizard of Oz*:

> I would while away the hours
> Conversing with the flowers
> If I only had a brain.

Anyway, we talked about it. Talking helps. We began very early, and we have never stopped. Years ago now, I bought Matt a book called *The Child's Book about Brain Injury* by an M.D., Richard A. Gardner. I first read it to Matthew when he was about seven years old. He knew as well as I did that he was different; he might as well try to understand his differences and come to terms with them.

When Matt was about eight years old, he had to have his tonsils out (for the second time). I took him to the hospital the afternoon before his scheduled surgery, and my husband and I went back that evening to see him before his bedtime. He was having a very good time. There were new friends to meet and play with, and a whole playroom full of new toys that he wanted to show us. As he scampered down the hall ahead of us, old Killjoy Mom said to him, "Remember, Matt, you're not here only for fun and games. You're going to have your tonsils out in the morning."

"Not me," said Matt, and pointed to one of the kids in the playroom. "That other guy!"

The point is that you tell your child about his operations and what to expect; you tell him why he has a sore throat, or how long you think the measles is going to last. Why not, then, be as honest and straightforward as you can about brain injury, developmental handicap, whatever you want to call it? You are not going to cause any more pain than he will suffer at the hands of other people, and your honesty may help to arm him.

There is a technical phrase for the credibility gap that occurs when a person (parent) says one thing and does another. It's called "cognitive dissonance." It can be excessive praise for a simple task badly performed, coupled by a refusal to allow another attempt or by a duplication of the work ("Let Mommy do that, she's faster"). Either way, the kid knows he's been had. The same cognitive dissonance occurs when a child is assured he is perfectly all right but all his senses tell him he is not. Much better to call a spade a spade and figure out how to work with it, even though the ground is rock-hard.

The sad, inexorable fact is that you have to keep on identifying that spade for what it is. Brain injury doesn't go away. The rosy future never comes, not the way it happens in fairy-tales or in other normal people's lives. Boots never wins the princess or the kingdom. Life for a handicapped person keeps on being difficult, keeps on presenting hardships and obstacles and anguish and pain. They never stop. At some time in the growing-up process, that realization comes home fully.

On Matt's twenty-first birthday, I had a small dinner party for him with his girlfriend Sandy and a couple of his closest friends with their girlfriends. They didn't want to do anything special after dinner (which was special), just sit and listen to records and talk. But they had a good time. When the evening was over, I drove Sandy home. Matt sat in the back seat with her while I acted as chauffeur. I could hear their conversation, though I didn't comment. I heard Matt say, after he had mused aloud for a moment at having reached the heady age of twenty-one, "Don't you wish you were normal?"

"What do you mean?" asked Sandy. She is less normal, that is, not as bright as he is, so she is spared the pain of comparison. Matt didn't pursue the conversation, but it haunted me: *If I only had a brain*.

Oddly enough, Matthew has a better brain than most people give him credit for. His wonderful teachers at Kohai found a few keys to unlocking it, and he made wonderful progress in his two years at that school. He earned three grade-nine credits and his school director deemed him ready to attempt an adult upgrading course, in which he was duly enrolled. He was to start there in the fall of 1983. A week after his last day at Kohai, Matt was admitted to Queen Street Mental Health Centre, in full flight again.

He was frightened by his success, frightened that he might have to repeat it, that it might be expected of him. He was frightened of his future, fearful of change, and scared, too, I think, that the new school might turn out to be like that hated boarding school. Once again he went through the anger, the hallucinations, the anxiety. Once again he was shifting from foot to foot, in the grip of Haldol. But this time he was angry at being locked up as well, and angry at having allowed his state to go that far. He responded quickly to medication and was out in a month, marvelling at the care he had received. I marvelled, too.

The support system of MTAMR, specifically of his counsellors, was wonderful. In fact, it was so efficient that I felt left out, until I realized how fortunate I was. I know now that if (and when) anything happens to me, there is care for Matthew.

He was released in a month. The drugs began to be reduced, under the care of a psychiatrist. He was better in time to start the new school. But it was a tough summer. As I say, problems don't go away. Just when you think you're in the clear, something else hits you. Be grateful for a plateau. Soon enough you have to start climbing again, pushing that old eightball up hill.

What you have been striving for, all his life, is normality. You want to see your children carry on the normal rhythms of life as you have known it, of the days, the weeks, the years, the entire life-cycle, with its growing up, its cleaving together, its thrust into the future with a new generation. You hope for certain economic standards — at least normal housing and a place within the community. Perhaps you fear isolation most of all. We all do.

The real handicap, as the years go on, is the isolation, the lack of a peer group. The handicapped have so few friends. As family dwindles away, the parents aging or dead, the siblings married, moved away, intent on their own lives and families, the handicapped person finds himself more and more isolated. His closest companion is the television set. Again, this is where a support group becomes more and more important. If you can leave your damaged child a circle of people on whom he can count for friendship and assistance in adulthood, that is a wonderful legacy.

All his life you've been asking yourself, "What's to become of him?" Now the future is here and it keeps on keeping on – stretching ahead bleakly with as many obstacles as there ever were. You've run out of magic wands, and "cures" are a thing of the past. You and he have long since accepted his limitations and resigned yourselves to coping within them. He still doesn't read well, if at all. His penmanship and spelling are abysmal, if he can write. He loses things, still gets mixed up about instructions, and occasionally gets lost. He's just not very organized. If he has a job, it's not very interesting. And now he's growing older.

What of the distant future? Handicapped people are living longer now, thanks to modern medical care and good nutrition. We are facing a generation of geriatric handicapped people, of aged and aging perhaps multiply handicapped people, no longer belligerent sons and hidden daughters. Their parents will be long gone. Where will they go? I'll tell you right now, no nursing home wants them. There are waiting lists as it is for the senior citizens' homes in this country of institutions. We're going to have to face the prospect of group homes for aging m.r. people very soon. They will need specialized day programs, since they will be too old even for the make-work projects of the sheltered workshops; they will need special diets; and they will need make-believe relatives, if they have no next-of-kin left. What's to become of them all?

I found out about one program in London, Ontario, called Future Watch. It is an attempt to watch over the future of the aging handicapped. We are going to need many more such advocacy programs in the future.

This is a book about learning disability, not the meaning of life, but I'll tell you something. My son Matthew smiles. He has given and received a lot of love in his lifetime. He makes people feel good. When he was withdrawn from me, as he was during his two breakdowns, I realized how dependent I was on him, for his unfailing patience, support, willingness, and good humour. Truly, he is a successful human being, and his life has meaning. I believe every life has meaning.

"It's not easy," I said to Matt once during one of our talks. (I must have said it more than once!)

"Nothing is, is it?" he replied.

We had been discussing a project very dear to my heart. I have been working on a musical inspired by Matt's life. I call it *Boy in a Cage*. Even the title was inspired by Matt. When he was six he went to see a children's play of mine called *Kingsayer*. In one scene in a school playground, the Kingsayer boy works a magic incantation on a secondary character, a mean type who deserves it.

> Cross-patch,
> Draw the latch—
> And don't come out until the end of recess.

The meanie is trapped by this and spends recess patting around the sides of an invisible prison he can't escape from. Matt came home from the play and told me about the "boy in a cage." I realized how meaningful the image was to him, and it has never left me.

Anyway, we were discussing it because I was finally trying to get something down on paper, and I needed Matt's help. He has his own wisdom and clarity and sometimes a simplicity and power of expression that I cannot duplicate. I asked him about growing up.

"I'm still a little kid, in some ways," he said. "Not as in age— but you can act different ages."

He knows that, you see, the difference between his chronological age and the age that his competence and appearance bestow on him. Most people think Matt is about seventeen. He is twenty-two, will be twenty-three by the time this book is out.

I asked how he felt when he was sad.

"I feel lonely," he said. "What do I do with lonely? I try to be unlonely."

Thinking of the Scarecrow, I asked him about wishes.

"A wish," said Matthew, "is a thing that you wish something would come true, and if it doesn't come true—that's a wish." He knows there are no fairy-godmothers in this world, no magic wand to change reality.

I wasn't probing to be unkind or to expose him. I wanted him to give me insights into my—our—hero Jason, the Boy in a Cage. So I asked him,

"Would you like to be born again?"

"Probably not," he said. "I'm okay as I am."

My friend Pat Capponi says that no one is born without a reason. We may have trouble seeing it, but there is a reason. I can see the reason for Matt's life in terms of mine and my family's. He was our cement, the glue in our family structure, our bright spot, our centrepiece. He taught us more about love than we might ever have known. All very well for us, nice for us to have him, but was that God's intent, to damage Matthew to make the rest of us appreciate our lives more?

"God is subtle," said Einstein, "but not malicious."

I suppose all we can do is accept the mystery. As I said, the older I get, the less I understand.

"I'm okay as I am," says Matthew, my son, in whom I am well pleased.

GLOSSARY

Agraphia – the inability to write words.

Aphasia – the inability to express oneself through speech, writing or signs, and/or the inability to understand spoken or written language due to injury or disease of certain brain centres.

Apraxia – difficulty performing a skilled or complex movement or series of movements, and the impaired ability to motor-plan.

Articulation – a term referring to the quality of speech, the clarity of sounds in speech.

Auditory Discrimination – the ability to hear the differences and similarities among and between sounds. Poor discrimination interferes with the ability to spell and to receive spoken language.

Auditory Memory – the process of remembering what is heard.

Auditory Sequencing – the ability to remember sequences of numbers such as a phone number after hearing it, or a sentence.

Bilateral Integration – the fine working relationship between the two sides of the body.

Body Image – an awareness of one's own body, and the relationship of the body parts to each other and position in space.

Central Nervous System – refers to the brain, and spinal cord.

Cerebral Dominance – the development of sidedness and the consistent preference for the use of a hand, foot, ear and eye.

Closure – the ability to construct a whole from its parts to complete an act or thought.

Coordination – the harmonious movement of the muscles of the body in the performance of habitual or complex movement.

Crossed Dominance – a condition in which the preferred eye, hand or foot are not on the same side of the body.

Decoding – the ability to take in symbols through the eyes (visual), or the ears (auditory) and derive meaning.

Discrimination – the ability to discriminate between different visual, auditory, or tactual (touch) signals.

Dyscalculia – the inability to do simple mathematics.

Dysfunction – impaired or lack of function.

Dysgraphia – the inability to write neatly or clearly.

Expressive Language – refers to language output through speech, writing, or gesture. A marked discrepancy between writing and speaking ability may indicate a learning disability.

Eye-Hand Coordination – the ability to synchronize the working of eye and hand in motor activities. This skill is necessary to many tasks such as sports, eating, and copying from the blackboard.

Feedback – the ability to self-monitor movement and information. It is also used to refer to the response we elicit from others as the result of our own behaviour.

Figure-Ground Discrimination – the ability to sort out important information from the overall, or background environment.

Fine Motor – the ability to use small muscles for precision tasks, such as the fingers in buttoning and writing.

Gross Motor – refers to large muscle groups used in such activities as skipping and physical exercise.

Integration – refers to the brain's ability to process information coming in from many sensory channels at the same time.

Kinesthesis – feedback from body movements and the ability to be aware of these movements and one's position in space. A dysfunction in this area causes distortion in perception and learning, and possible emotional side effects.

Laterality – internal awareness that the body has two sides, and discrimination between the sides for movement and directionality.

Left Hemisphere – the side of the brain which deals with language-related functions, such as spelling, writing, reading and comprehending.

Mixed Cerebral Dominance – a term to indicate that right or left handedness or dominance has not been established.

Mnemonic Devices – methods to assist memory.

Modality – a sensory pathway by which we receive information, i.e. sight.

Oculomotor – eye movements.

Organicity – a term referring to organic causes of learning and behavioural deficits, and denoting neurological impairment of difference.

Perception – the ability of the brain to receive and make sense of information from the senses.

Perceptual Motor Problem – inadequate functioning of the perceptual process integrated with motor processes, i.e. eye-hand coordination.

Perseveration – continued repetition of words or motions to a degree which annoys or puzzles adults and/or the inability to shift from one activity to another.

Phonics – a method of teaching reading by associating sounds with letters or groups of letters, as opposed to the whole-word method wherein the word is taught as one unit.

Psychomotor – the relationship between the brain and the muscles.

Receptive Language – generally refers to understanding the spoken word and how the brain processes language input.

Reversals – errors appearing in reading and writing, reversing the order of double-digit numbers, single letters, p, b, d, q; or letters within words (*pat* for *tap*).

Right Hemisphere – the side of the brain which has a visual-spatial function, memory for places and faces, creative ability and intuitive reasoning.

Self-Concept – an individual's opinion of himself/herself.

Spatial Discrimination – being able to discriminate between up and down, top and bottom, front and back, over and under, etc. Also refers to a difficulty in judging distances, and placement of objects.

Syndrome – a set of symptoms which occur together and make a discernable pattern.

Visual Acuity – keenness of vision.

Visual Discrimination – the process of detecting by sight, differences in objects or forms.

Visualization – the ability to picture, "in the mind's eye", objects, experiences, concepts, etc. during sensory input or following it.

Visual Memory – the ability to remember what things look like after exposure to them, such as words.

(from *Communique*, the newsletter published four times a year by Ontario Association for Children with Learning Disabilities)

BIBLIOGRAPHY

Bach, Richard. *Jonathan Livingston Seagull*. New York: The Macmillan Company, 1970.

Busch, Phyllis S. *A Walk in the Snow*. Philadelphia, New York: J.B. Lippincott Company, 1971.

The Celdic Report. A National Study of Canadian Children with Emotional and Learning Disorders, published by Leonard Crainford for The Commission on Emotional and Learning Disorders in Children, Canada, 1970.

Cruickshank, William M. *The Brain-Injured Child in Home, School, and Community*. Syracuse, New York: Syracuse University Press, 1967.

Doman, Glenn. *How to Teach Your Baby to Read*. New York: Random House, 1964.

Gardner, Richard. *The Child's Book about Brain Injury*. New York Association for Brain Injured Children, 1966.

Grollman, Earl A. *Explaining Death to Children*. Boston: Beacon Press, 1967.

Holt, John. *How Children Learn*. New York: Dell Publishing Company, 1967.

Jackson, Edgar N. *Telling a Child About Death*. New York: Channel Press, 1965.

Kauffman, Carol, and Farrell, Patricia. *If You Live With Little Children*. New York: G.P. Putnam's Sons, 1957.

Kratoville, Betty. *Listen, My Children, and You Shall Hear*. Danville, Illinois: The Interstate Printers & Publishers, 1968.

Kronick, Doreen. *They Too Can Succeed*. San Rafael, California: Academic Therapy Publications, 1969.

Kunc, Norman. *Ready Willing and Disabled*. Toronto: Personal Library, 1981.

Noyes, Joan, and Macneill, Norma. *Your Child Can Win*. Toronto: Macmillan of Canada, 1982.

Montessori, Maria. *The Montessori Method*. New York: Schocken Books, 1964.

Perske, Robert and Perske, Martha (illustrator). *New Life in The Neighbourhood: How Persons with Retardation or other Disabilities Can Help Make a Good Community Better*. Nashville: Abingdon, 1981.

Platt, Kin. *Hey, Dummy*. New York: Dell Publishing Company, 1974.

Putnam, Marie. *Mentely Handicapped Love*. Madiera Park, B.C.: Harbour Publishing, 1981.

Radler, D.H. with Kephart, Dr. Newell C. *Success Through Play*. New York & Evanston: Harper & Row, 1960.

Raskin, Ellen. *The Mysterious Disappearance of Leon*. New York: E.P. Dutton & Co., Inc., 1971.

————, *Spectacles*. Bloomfield, Conn./Toronto: Atheneum/McClelland and Stewart, 1968.

Shack, Sybil. *Armed with a Primer*. Toronto: McClelland and Stewart, 1965.

Vogel, Linda Jane. *Helping a Child Understand Death*. Philadelphia: Fortress Press, 1975.

Wolfensberger, Wolf. *The Origin and Nature of Our Institutional Models*. Syracuse, N.Y.: Human Policy Press, 1975.

Young, Marjabelle, and Buchwald, Ann. *Stand Up, Shake Hands, Say "How Do You Do."* New York: David McKay Co., Inc., 1969.

Zebroff, Kareen & Peter. *Yoga for Happier Children*. Vancouver: Fforbez Enterprises Ltd., 1973.

Other Useful Information:

Communique, newsletter published 4 times a year by
Ontario Association for Children with Learning Disabilities,
1901 Yonge Street, Suite 504,
Toronto, Ontario M4S 2Z3

Developmental Learning Materials Comprehensive Catalogue
PMB Industries Ltd.,
1220 Ellesmere Road,
Units 15-17,
Scarborough, Ontario M1P 2X5

Future Watch,
Jim Kidd,
77 Ranchwood Crescent,
London, Ontario N6G 3A1

Parents Learning Kit,
Epilepsy Association, Metro Toronto,
Ste. 214, 214 King Street West,
Toronto, Ontario M5H 1K4

People First,
c/o Ontario Association for the Mentally Retarded,
1367 Bayview Avenue,
Toronto, Ontario M4G 3A3
(483-4348)

Printed in Canada